The Lazy Cook

Book 1: Quick And Easy Meatless Meals

Susie Kelly

blackbird

Blackbird Digital Books
London 2015
The moral right of the author has been asserted.
Cover artwork © David Lewis www.davidlewiscartoons.com
Cover design by Fena Lee www.pheeena.carbonmade.com
ISBN-13: 97880993092251

25.12.2015

Very Merry Christmas
Ren

For Rob — No it's
NOT!
It's FOR
Renda

WITH ALL MY Looovies

MIKE.

Contents

Introduction

Well hello, and welcome! I'm so pleased you could make it. Do sit down and make yourself comfortable – tip the cat off the chair.

I apologise for the state of the kitchen; I'm a messy cook.

I hope I can show you that we eat very well despite not eating meat, and you won't find any nut roasts or soya substitutes here. Just because we live in France, we don't eat exclusively French food. French country cooking is generally meat-heavy – *cassoulet, coq au vin, boeuf bourguignon*. We like food with strong powerful flavours like Parmesan cheese, garlic, truffles (not the chocolate ones), capers, and spices, so Mediterranean and Indian cuisines are favourites. When I have spare time I'll happily spend all day in the kitchen creating multi-course meals, but those occasions are rare, and more often than not I look at the clock and think, oops, nearly lunch time, what shall we have? With my butterfly mind – one minute trotting off to prune the lavender, the next deciding to do the ironing, write a few chapters of a new book, phone a friend or play with the dogs, when mealtimes arrive I like recipes I can put together with a minimum fuss – no spun-sugar domes with pink smoke and silver bubbles floating around in it, and no smears, blobs, jus or foams (as somebody remarked once, it looks as if chef has spat on the plate).

This collection is the accumulation of decades of scribbled notes on backs of envelopes, tatty exercise books, recipes given to me by friends and vague recollections. I am always losing track of things, so I thought it was time to put everything in one place where I could find it quickly instead of hunting through drawers and cupboards. This is my personal collection of fail-safe quick and easy recipes for friends and family, which you are welcome to share. None of them require very much time or skill to prepare, and they make no claim to be haute cuisine, just wholesome recipes that anybody can follow.

There are numerous variations of most of them. I enjoy watching foodies and chefs giving a new twist to old favourites, and I enjoy trying them, but sometimes I think they go too far and the originals lose the identity that I loved in the first place. For me there's a great deal of nostalgia connected to the food we eat.

I have never 'turned' a vegetable, nor am I ever likely to. For a start, it seems so wasteful, and secondly because I probably could not if my life depended upon it. I am not cut out to do fiddly food. I'm far too impatient to whittle carrots into scale replicas of the Orient Express or to peel and stuff grapes. I am hopelessly ham-fisted and fiddly doesn't suit my modus operandi. Neither do recipes with multiple columns of ingredients covering two pages of instructions. When we want to eat high-end food, beautifully presented, we go out and let the professionals do the hard work.

When I'm really short of time, fast food in our house is beans on toast, cheese on toast, Welsh rarebit or fried egg sandwiches. If you want to invite me for a meal, feed me a baked potato, with crispy almost-burned skin, served with a knob of butter or covered with melted cheese and I'll be ecstatic.

Except where specifically mentioned, the quantities given are not written in stone and do not require atomic precision. A little more or less of most ingredients won't make an enormous difference to the finished result. If there's an ingredient you don't like, then unless it is essential leave it out, or substitute something else. I'm one of those people who believe that fats are good for you, so I'm generous with them. You can always reduce the quantities to suit yourself.

I have indicated whether each recipe is vegan and/or gluten-free for the benefit of those who aren't certain, and have flagged up a 'raw egg' warning. It's quite disheartening when you think you have carefully prepared a meal for somebody with an intolerance or allergy, and discover at the last minute that you've accidentally included an ingredient that they can't eat. Of course, you can always substitute margarine or oil for butter in most recipes, although it will alter the taste somewhat.

To simplify measurements, I've converted Imperial and metric measurements wherever possible into cups and spoons. I find a set of stainless steel measuring cups and spoons, which are as cheap as chips and take up almost no space, more practical and quicker than weighing everything on kitchen scales – which I've found to my cost in the past to be not always reliable.

The volume of my measuring cup is 300 ml, equivalent to 10 US fluid ounces, or 10.5 Imperial fluid ounces – about the capacity of a normal teacup.

Flours differ; egg sizes differ; oven temperatures differ; spoon sizes differ. What is under-seasoned for one person is too salty for another. If something doesn't turn out quite the way you hope, it's always worth having another go and tweaking the recipe to see if there's a solution.

1

How I Began Cooking

Being brought up and living for many years in Kenya, I was spoiled by a wonderful African cook who could give any Michelin-starred chef a run for his money. He cooked traditional British food – from full English breakfasts to Sunday roasts – including the lightest, fluffiest, puffiest Yorkshire puddings – as well as superb, authentic Italian and Indian dishes. He was truly passionate about cooking and sang, whistled and hummed happily to himself in the kitchen where I was completely surplus to requirements.

Moving to live in England was a shock, coming home from work to not only do my own housework, but also cook for a family of four. For a while we ate pot noodles reconstituted with boiling water, tinned pies, frozen meals cooked in the microwave, and powdered desserts whisked into milk. I had no idea how to prepare food from scratch.

I started thinking about nutrition seriously the day I saw tomatoes for sale that were advertised as 'grown for flavour'. Well, what a novel idea! And I began looking at the additives in the processed products we were eating, and wondering what they did, and why they were necessary. Particularly flavour enhancers. Why did manufacturers need to put flavour into the food? Didn't it have any in the first place? There were E numbers and polysyllabic unpronounceable ingredients. I visualised them coming out vats and wondered if I would want to eat them if they were served on a spoon. The cost of processed food and their long lists of mysterious contents was alarming, so I thought I'd better start learning an alternative way to feed the family.

Watching formidable Fanny Cradock, amiable Galloping Gourmet Graham Kerr and ebullient Keith Floyd displaying their skills on the television inspired me. It looked so easy! I bought a simple cookery book and began experimenting with chops, sausages, home-made chips, and soon, somewhat to my surprise, managed to produce a perfectly roasted chicken with roast potatoes, Vichy carrots and Brussels sprouts – the first complete meal I had ever made from scratch. I realised that with time and guidance, cooking wasn't rocket science.

Always one to gallop before I could trot, I tried a fully boned, stuffed and reconstructed chicken. After an hour of gory wrestling, a kitchen surface spattered with fleshy globs, and two sliced fingertips, the result looked like an albino frog that had been dropped from a great height and landed on a rock.

Following a recipe for Yorkshire pudding, I made the batter and put it in the fridge for half an hour as instructed, while the dish of fat heated up in the oven. When I poured the batter into the dish, I did not expect it to erupt like a volcano, spewing a molten mess all over the kitchen. Nowhere had the cookery book mentioned that Pyrex dishes, being made of glass, would not stand up to the shock of chilled batter hitting spattering oil.

Then there was the great icing sugar misunderstanding. I wanted to make a simple glacé icing, just a mixture of icing sugar and water with a splash of lemon juice. The recipe gave the quantity of sugar, and said: 'Mix with sufficient water to coat the back of a spoon'. As ridiculous as this sounds, I took it literally, and tried to see how much water I could balance on the back of a spoon, using progressively larger spoons in the hope that if I found one large enough, it would hold enough water to mix the icing. Either I was particularly obtuse, or the instructions were badly phrased. Sometimes following recipes is not enough – you need to apply a pinch of common sense.

Over the years, I *think* I've made every mistake it's possible to make in the kitchen, including pouring hot oil back into a plastic bottle and watching the bottle transform into a distorted mess before sinking gently into nothingness, flooding the surface, units and floor with a sticky mess which took months to remove.

2

A Few Words About Sandy

Imagine that you are invited to dinner, and that when you arrive, you are expected to cook the food yourself.

When I lived in rural England many years ago, every so often I'd come across injured wildlife. Generally I would take them to our local vet who always treated these creatures free of charge. On a Sunday walk, one of our dogs startled a young pheasant. Before it could become airborne, they snatched at it and brought it back to me. The bird was shocked, but seemed otherwise uninjured, until I put it down on the ground, when it was clear that it had an injured leg. I phoned a local wildlife sanctuary, who suggested that I take it to a lady who would be able to care for and repair it.

I phoned the number they had given me, and a cut-glass British accent replied: "Yes?" Just that. No niceties. Wondering if I'd called a wrong number, I mentioned the injured bird. "Bring it round." She snapped out her address and hung up. I folded the pheasant into a cardboard box with some straw, and drove down a bumpy track to a rather dilapidated house at the end of a driveway hedged by rampant brambles. There was a garage to one side, where something was snorting loudly. I thought I must have mistaken the address, because it did not match the top-drawer upper-class English accent.

A very small woman in a bedraggled waterproof jacket, tweed cap and spectacles with a cracked lens came towards the car.

"Pheasant?" she said, turning her back on me and walking towards the house. At the door she turned and beckoned me. "Well come on, what are you waiting for?"

With the box tucked under my arm I followed her through the door into a gloomy hallway piled with old newspapers and sacks of animal food, into the kitchen, where every surface was covered in cages and boxes with perforated lids from which came squeaks, mews, chirps and rustling noises.

She lifted out the pheasant, which twisted its head round and pecked at her spectacles. "Yes," she murmured, "good bird."

The good bird sat placidly on the kitchen table while she manipulated its legs. "Dislocated hip," she said, putting it back in the box. "Just takes time and rest. And they have a high pain threshold, so don't worry." To demonstrate its pain threshold, the pheasant pushed open the lid of the box and scrambled back onto the table.

Thanking her, I turned to leave. "Come for supper," she called. "Wednesday week. Seven o'clock. You can see how the patient's doing. Dress down."

That was how I met Sandy. And over the following three years I spent many evenings in her kitchen, usually with a collection of waifs, strays and lame ducks, both animal and human. Meals were always chaotic, because she never managed to find time to cook them herself. Either she was poulticing a hoof or feeding baby hedgehogs with a dropper, keeping an orphaned baby rabbit warm in her cleavage or something else that took priority over cooking. It was down to the guests to prepare the meal, clearing an area on the kitchen table, rummaging through the larder, digging out recipes from toppling piles of books, magazines and newspaper cuttings. Whatever your rank – the vicar and his wife, the local MP, the man from the council who drove the road cleaner, you all mucked in one way or another. It was tremendous fun, wonderfully random and unpredictable.

While her guests were deciding what to cook, Sandy, putting a basket of kittens or box of ducklings under a heat lamp would say: "Now come on chaps, let's just have something sensible. Don't go mucking it about. Less is more." I'm inclined to agree with her, because I am not overly keen on immensely complicated dishes that lose their identity in a maze of drizzles and blobs of different flavours.

Although she didn't like having her food 'mucked about' and preferred simple dishes, Sandy had a particularly sweet tooth and love of indulgent desserts, feeling as I do that if you're going to have a pudding, go the whole way and have a good one.

Whenever I make a rich creamy dessert, I can hear Sandy saying: "Oh for heaven sake, must we eat this stuff?" – and remember her filling her plate and scraping it clean.

3

"Go ask Caesar what he wants in his salad."

Salads

According to the Oxford dictionary: 'A cold dish of various mixtures of raw or cooked vegetables, usually seasoned with oil, vinegar or other dressing and sometimes accompanied by meat, fish or other ingredients'.

"We're going to Auntie Ellen for tea," were words to chill the heart in summer. Because tea in summer at Auntie Ellen's meant salad. (In the winter it was stew.)

Undoubtedly healthy – there were no supermarkets in those days, no genetically-engineered foodstuffs, and amongst our class at the time, no refrigerators. Housewives shopped daily from small local stores – the butcher, baker, fishmonger and greengrocer, or the street market stalls, so food was always fresh and locally grown. No produce came from further than a few miles away.

Auntie Ellen – she was actually a great aunt and in my eyes unbelievably old – walked the half-mile to market on Saturday morning to buy the best and freshest ingredients for our Sunday salad, which never varied: lettuce, tomatoes, radishes, beetroot, cucumber, spring onion, and celery that she kept in a glass of salted water, served with slices of slippery pink ham, and bread and butter. On a good day this was followed by junket, blancmange or ice-cream with tinned fruit salad, and on a bad day by jelly that shuddered as it was cut and lay quivering in terror on my plate, which I found very disturbing because it looked as if it was alive.

Auntie Ellen regarded her salad as a treat. I'd sooner have had a slap. I didn't greatly like celery or cucumber or lettuce, or beetroot or radishes, but was brought up to eat what was given to me. 'Not liking' something was not an option. The war (second, not first) had only finished a few years earlier, and many foods were in short supply – things like bacon, sugar, eggs and butter were strictly rationed. Housewives had to find ways to create dishes out of ingredients that were never intended for the purpose and to stretch them to feed everybody. Young and old had dug up their gardens to grow their own fruit and vegetables – 'Digging for Victory' was the slogan. You graciously ate what you were given and were truly grateful for it. Not only were there people dying from starvation, it was considered unforgivably ill-mannered to refuse any food offered when you were a guest. That is something I find odd today, when people poke, sniff or dig about suspiciously in their food or scrape things to the side of their plate. It simply wasn't allowed, unless you had an allergy to something.

There were other rules of etiquette, some at home and some at school – at boarding school we had broom handles inserted between our elbows to make us sit up straight at table – and not all of them have stood the test of time.

Elbows off the table. Put your knife and fork down when chewing. Don't speak with your mouth full. Don't speak at all during mealtimes. Put your shoulders back. Don't mash your peas to make them easier to manage. Tilt your soup bowl away from you, and sip from the edge of the spoon. Don't make slurpy noises when eating. Don't make any noise at all when eating. Do not cut your food into pieces and then eat it with a fork. Don't blow on hot food. Leave your knife and fork neatly beside each other when you've finished. Clean every speck of food from your plate. Leave some for Mr Manners. Do not touch your food with your fingers. Do not scrape your knife and fork on your plate. Don't tilt your chair back. And so on, and on.

In fact there were so many rules that many meals were rather an ordeal, waiting to be told off for not doing, or doing something incorrectly, but they eventually became second nature. Until I met the Italians. When it came to mealtimes, the idea was to enjoy the food, not to impress people with your good manners. I don't mean they were ill-mannered, far from it, but they ate with gusto and abandon. A forkful of pasta waved in the air to emphasise a point; bread used to mop up sauces; cutlery left higgledy-piggledy on the plate; loud talking, forks used to scoop up recalcitrant peas; soup eaten from the front of the bowl; elbows all over the place. I felt like a prig. Food is to be eaten with joy, was the message. And so yes, at home or with close friends, I prop my elbows on the table, eat my chips with my fingers, abandon my knife when a fork alone will do, dip my bread in soup and use it to mop my plate clean. I draw the line at talking with my mouth full and making slurpy noises. :) And there are times and places when the old rules kick in out of respect for those who stick to them.

Apart from meat, undercooked fish or undercooked egg white, I'll try almost anything. Because if you don't try it, how do you know whether or not you're going to like it? I don't understand people who decide they don't like something before they've tried it, and I know of four friends who had always sworn they would never eat garlic and who, when tasting garlic bread for the first time (without knowing what it was) fell in love with it. My darling daughter was the most difficult child to feed, refusing to try anything she hadn't eaten before and therefore living on an extremely limited diet. She was twelve

13

years old before she cautiously decided to taste Chinese food, and instantly fell in love with it. All those years wasted! On the other hand my son could be guaranteed to always order the most expensive and exotic dish on the menu; he takes after me.

Encouraged by friends, I have tried many times to like sushi, and failed. But at least I tried and if I had to eat it I would.

Getting back to Auntie Ellen's wholesome salad, the problem was that it didn't have any dressing apart from a sprinkle of vinegar. It was a plateful of colourful damp stuff. Each ingredient had its own distinctive flavour, but there was nothing to hold them together until Auntie Ellen overcame her natural suspicion of anything processed and, encouraged by my mother, bought a bottle of Heinz Salad Cream. True, she only dribbled one teaspoonful over each plate, but that small dab transformed the collection of wet cubes and slices into something quite different. The flavours blended and complemented each other, and Auntie Ellen's salad became almost enjoyable. I still struggled with lettuce as it was damp and floppy and tasted bitter. I confided in my mother, who came up with the idea of sprinkling it with sugar, which gave it crunch and overcame the bitterness, and once in a while I still eat it like that, even if only to take me back to those early childhood days.

We usually have a salad at least once a day, because it's quick and easy to prepare from fresh and/or store cupboard ingredients, and incredibly versatile. It's also the perfect answer to unexpected guests turning up - it takes almost no time to get a salad on the table, and if you have some cheese, a tin of fish and some good bread, it's a meal in itself. Auntie Ellen's traditional salad is a distant memory. Here are some of the ingredients I use, experimenting with combinations of flavours and textures, and dressings ranging from rich mayonnaise to vinegars – balsamic, red wine, fruit-flavoured (Lidl do some particularly gorgeous apricot, pear and apple-flavoured balsamic vinegars in their DeLuxe range, as well as affordable, luxurious truffle oil), extra virgin olive oils, nut oils, vegan mayonnaise (recipe in Sauces and Pickles section) or why not a good dollop of Heinz Salad Cream?

Anchovies
Artichoke hearts
Avocado
Beetroot
Bulghur
Capers
Carrots
Cauliflower
Celeriac
Cheese - grated, cubed, crumbled
Chickpeas
Chillies
Chopped apple or pear (keep in water with lemon juice until serving to stop from turning brown)
Cooked or tinned fish
Cooked pasta
Cooked peas
Cooked potato
Cooked rice
Couscous
Croutons
Cucumber
Dried fruits
Finely chopped garlic
Finely sliced Brussels sprouts
Finely sliced onions
Finely sliced raw cabbage
Fresh herbs
Fried onions
Gherkins
Grapes
Green beans
Hard-boiled egg
Kidney beans

15

Kiwi fruit
Lentils
Lettuce
Mango
Mushrooms
Olives
Palm hearts
Peaches
Peanuts
Pickled onions
Pine nuts
Pomegranate seeds
Preserved lemons
Pumpkin seeds
Quinoa
Red peppers, fresh or bottled
Sesame seeds
Sliced banana
Sultanas
Sun-dried tomatoes
Sunflower seeds
Sweetcorn
Tinned pineapple
Tomatoes. An unripe tomato is an abomination, tough and tasteless with a woody core and no juice. It doesn't look good and it doesn't smell good. It also doesn't taste good. I expect there are all kinds of clever things to be done with unripe tomatoes, but they don't belong in salads. NEVER keep tomatoes in the fridge. It breaks their hearts and crushes their spirit, and all their flavour falls out.
Walnuts

The great lettuce debate
I heard quite a heated debate about whether to cut or tear lettuce. For heaven sake, it's only a lettuce! I really do not like it served in great big pieces. It's unwieldy and to eat it politely you need to try and fold it up into a neat parcel with a knife and

fork. I prefer to shred it quite finely with a knife which, if you do it at the last minute, does not cause the edges of the lettuce to brown, and is more attractive visually and easier to eat.

Tzatziki

This brings back memories of Greek holidays, sitting on a vine-covered terrace with a glass of chilled wine, a bowl of olives, a chunk of feta cheese and a loaf of fresh-baked bread, and feeling the warmth of the sun on my skin.

Grate or chop very finely one peeled cucumber, then sprinkle well with salt and leave in a colander over a bowl for half an hour to drain off excess liquid.

Rinse well, press out any water, and then stir the cucumber into 1 cup of Greek yoghurt or fromage blanc, with a very finely chopped or crushed clove of garlic, salt and pepper to taste, and either a heaped teaspoon of mint sauce, or a tablespoon of finely chopped fresh mint.

Chill before serving.
Gluten free

Raita

Similar to tzatziki, yet quite different. While it's ideally served as a side dish with curries, we also enjoy it as a light snack, accompanied by chapatti or naan bread.

Grate or very finely chop a peeled cucumber, sprinkle well with salt and leave in a colander over a bowl to drain for half an hour.

Meanwhile beat ¾ cup of yoghurt or fromage blanc with a pinch of salt and a pinch of sugar until it thickens. Then stir in the rinsed and drained cucumber, a clove of crushed garlic, a good pinch of turmeric, a pinch of powdered cumin or garam masala, and a handful of chopped coriander, or mint. Chill to serve.

Variation: Add a small handful of raisins or sultanas
Gluten free

Pear and blue cheese salad
The sweetness of the pear contrasts nicely with the saltiness of the cheese in this simple salad.

You can either peel and poach fresh pears, or use well-drained tinned ones. Cut them into quarters, remove the core, and cut the quarters in half. Lay on a bed of lamb's lettuce or rocket, and crumble over a few ounces of blue cheese. Dress with 1 teaspoon of olive oil mixed with one teaspoon of balsamic vinegar.
Gluten free

Banana, peanut and spring onion salad
Colourful and crunchy.

Chop two large bananas and coat them with the juice of one orange or lemon. Add a handful of chopped spring onions, a finely chopped red or green pepper, and a handful of peanuts.

Bind it together with Greek yoghurt or mayonnaise, and chill well before serving on a bed of freshly-shredded lettuce.
Substitute vegan mayonnaise for vegan version, gluten free
Raw egg

Prawn, pepper and pineapple salad
Mix two cups of very fresh, cooked peeled prawns with a can of drained pineapple chunks, half a cup of chopped spring onions, a cupful of chopped fresh or bottled sweet red peppers, half a cucumber, diced and a tablespoon of parsley or mint.

Add sufficient mayonnaise to bind it together, and chill before serving on a bed of lettuce.

Substitute vegan mayonnaise for vegan version, gluten free
Raw egg

Panzanella - aka stale bread salad

Here in France the *boulangeries* are always happy to sell off cheaply their stale bread (baguettes have a very short life-span; if they're not eaten within a few hours of baking, they turn to stone). Many people buy these stale loaves to supplement their animal feed, but if you came from good peasant stock in Italy, when times were hard, there was no way anything was going to the livestock if there was a way it could be used for humans. Stale bread could be crushed into breadcrumbs for coating or thickening soup, cubed as an addition to a frittata, toasted as a base for bruschetta or crostini, or used as a salad ingredient to bulk out the vegetables. That's my favourite way, although the ends of stale baguettes go to our two pygmy goats, who love them.

Panzanella is one of those recipes where there's no right or wrong way to make it; you do it the way that suits you. There are many variations. This is how I make it.

The bread MUST BE stale, and it must 'proper' bread, not the processed sliced stuff. Sourdough works well, and any type of coarse, rustic loaf. If you use processed sliced bread, it will turn into a horrid, gluey mess. Just try soaking a piece in water for a few minutes and squeeze out the water to see the grey result. Ugh.

Cut the bread into cubes of about 1" (2.5cm), and put in a large bowl. Pour over enough water to cover, and leave for 10 minutes.

While the bread is soaking crush some garlic, chop some cucumber, celery and plenty of really red, ripe tomatoes, and slice some red onion finely. Quantities are up to you. Squeeze the water out of the bread.

Put everything into a salad bowl and mix well. The bread should be soft and crumbly. Dress with loads of olive oil and red wine vinegar, and season with salt and pepper. Turn it all over and leave for an hour or so at room temperature. To serve, sprinkle with torn basil leaves.

I sometimes add olives, capers, bits of anchovy, and once some pieces of feta cheese – but that's a secret. :)
Omit anchovies and cheese for vegans

Tuna salad
This classic, ever-popular recipe makes a good snack for two or a starter for four.

You need four hard-boiled eggs. (Remember that very fresh eggs are the most difficult to peel. They're easier if they are 4-5 days old. Put them in a pan of cold water, bring to the boil, set a timer for 10 minutes, then remove from the heat. Immediately tip away the water, and shake the eggs around in the saucepan so they crash together and the shells crack. Then fill the pan with cold water and set aside for 10 minutes. The shells should now peel off cleanly and easily.)

Mash the eggs with 1 cup of well-drained tinned tuna, 1/4 cup of softened butter and 2 tablespoons of double cream or mayonnaise. Season with salt and black pepper.

Spread on triangles of hot toast, sprinkle lightly with cayenne pepper, and serve with a quarter of a lemon.

I serve this with a small bowl of capers and gherkins so that those who like them (me!) can help themselves.
*For a gluten free version, replace the toast with crisp lettuce leaves. *Raw egg**

COOKED SALADS

Egg, tomato and potato salad

Judge quantities of ingredients according to how many servings you want. One tomato, one egg and two potatoes per person is a general guideline. Mix together quartered hard-boiled eggs, cold sliced boiled potatoes and skinned tomatoes. (Plunge very ripe tomatoes into the boiling water in which you are cooking the eggs, for 1 minute. When pricked with the point of a knife, the skin should start to split, and they can then be easily peeled.) It isn't essential to skin them, but I think it's nicer if you do. Under-ripened tomatoes, together with all their other faults, are nearly impossible to skin and will taste horrible with this dish.

Stir in sufficient mayonnaise (see recipe) to coat generously, sprinkle with chopped chives, and serve at room temperature.

This is quite a substantial salad that makes a satisfying light lunch. Extras can be added, like capers, olives or gherkins, or whatever else you fancy.
Substitute vegan mayonnaise for vegan version, gluten free
Raw egg*

Sicilian salad

A heavenly and robust new potato salad from Southern Italy. The following quantity should serve 4 people generously.

Cook a couple of pounds of potatoes in salted water until just tender and still firm – about 15 minutes. If using new potatoes, leave the skins on.

While the potatoes are cooking, whisk together 3 tablespoons of olive oil, 2 tablespoons of red wine vinegar, and 2 tablespoons of chopped sun-dried tomatoes. Season with salt and freshly-ground black pepper.

When the potatoes are cooked, chop them roughly and stir in the dressing while the potatoes are still hot.

Cut 15-20 cherry tomatoes in half and add to the potatoes together with the drained contents of a jar of grilled red peppers, roughly chopped.

Allow the salad to cool to room temperature before serving, adding a tablespoon of drained capers, a tablespoon of sliced baby gherkins and a handful of basil leaves, roughly torn.
Vegan, gluten free

Prawn and rice salad
This substantial rice-based salad makes a great dish for brunch, a picnic or buffet. The following quantity should serve 4-6.

Cook 1½ cups of long grain rice according to the directions on the packet. (With so many different types of long grain rice now, you need to check the cooking directions. The dish works best with simple long grain rather than the more delicate Basmati or Thai rices. Whatever you do, don't use round or risotto rice or the end result will be a sticky mess.)

Leave the rice to cool, then stir in 2 cups of cooked prawns, 1 cup of cooked peas, and 1 cup of sliced canned or bottled red peppers.

Shake together in a jar 4 teaspoons of oil, 4 teaspoons of red wine vinegar, 1 teaspoon of sugar, 1 teaspoon of mustard powder, ½ teaspoon of black pepper, 1 teaspoon of salt and one clove of crushed garlic.

Pour the dressing over the rice mixture, mix well, cover and leave in the fridge for a couple of hours or overnight for the flavours to develop. Garnished with a few prawns with their shells on and sprinkle with parsley

Meat-eaters could add or substitute cooked chicken pieces, or chorizo in place of or as well as the prawns.

Gluten free. For a vegan version, omit the prawns - it's still quite nice without them. You can replace them with cashew nuts.

Warm potato salad

Peel and boil potatoes in salted water until just cooked. Drain and roughly chop or mash; stir in a finely chopped onion, a handful of chopped chives, half a cup of chopped gherkins and/or capers. Bind with a generous quantity of mayonnaise, and serve immediately.

Substitute vegan mayonnaise for vegan version, gluten free
Raw egg

Tomato and mozzarella salad

The colours of the Italian flag represented in this beautifully simple and wonderfully tasty salad.

Slice some deep red ripe tomatoes crossways and sprinkle with a little salt. Top with a generous piece of fresh Mozzarella cheese and grind a dash of black pepper over it. Put a fresh basil leaf on each slice, and dribble over a few drops of olive oil. Serve immediately.

Gluten free

Indian onion salad

This makes a nice accompaniment to a main dish and is equally good on a buffet table.

For four servings slice up 4-5 medium onions very finely. Fry in a generous knob of butter, ghee or a glug of vegetable oil over a gentle heat, adding a teaspoon of curry powder. Continue cooking the onions until they soften, become transparent and begin to caramelise.

Add a handful of raisins or sultanas, a tablespoon of brown sugar, and 2 tablespoons of vinegar. Cook for a further 5 minutes over gentle heat, stirring to prevent sticking. Serve at room temperature.

Replace butter or ghee with vegetable oil for a vegan version, gluten free

Grilled aubergine salad

To serve 2 people, cut a large aubergine into 1" (2.5cm) thick circles, and lightly brush with olive oil. Place under a hot grill until they are a rich golden colour, then turn and repeat on the other side.

While they are cooking, chop some tomatoes (I generally skin mine, but it's not essential. If the tomatoes aren't ripe, you won't be able to anyway. Use tinned plum tomatoes if you can't get fresh ripe ones), and mix with some chopped red onions. Then add a mixture of olive oil, balsamic vinegar, a good pinch of salt and pepper, and a crushed clove of garlic. Pour over the grilled aubergines and leave at room temperature for an hour for the flavours to develop.

Vegan, gluten free

Niçoise salad

The iconic French Mediterranean salad is as controversial as it's delicious. There are the 'authentic' recipes beloved of classic French cooks, and other versions at which they turn up their Gallic noses.

Sometimes we have potatoes in ours, and sometimes we don't. Sometimes we include anchovies, and sometimes we don't. I say just make it the way you like it and let the food snobs have it their way. :) Essential ingredients are tuna, green beans, tomato, olives and hard-boiled egg.

When I make it, I use tinned tuna, fresh or frozen green beans cooked just long enough so that they still 'squeak' when bitten;

quartered peeled tomatoes or cherry tomatoes; quartered hard-boiled eggs, a few stoned black olives, and a couple of teaspoons of capers. If we have guests and they like anchovies, I'll add them too, but I don't think they are an essential ingredient – the olives add sufficient saltiness. You can also add finely sliced red onion rings, diced red pepper, and small new potatoes. So maybe it's not 'authentic' – but does that really matter? It tastes great however you make it.

For the dressing mix 4 tablespoons of olive oil, 4 tablespoons of red wine vinegar, 1 teaspoon of sugar, 1 teaspoon of mustard powder, ½ teaspoon of black pepper, 1 teaspoon of salt and one clove of crushed garlic.
Gluten free

4

Eggs

One of the wonders of the world, surely. A hermetically sealed, perfectly packed, portion of protein.

The eternal question of which did come first makes my brain spin. How can you have a chicken without having an egg, and how can you have an egg without having a chicken? Maybe creationists just accept that chickens were created with the in-built ability to reproduce by laying eggs (ovolution?), while evolutionists continue to seek an answer. To me it's the same as trying to contemplate infinity – more than my mind can entertain. And why is it always the chicken brought into question? What about ants, flies, ostriches, spiders - they too all begin life as eggs without being constantly questioned as to their origins. For the answer to the original question, we'll have to wait until science can come up with a definitive answer and explanation as to how any creature that is born from an egg could have been born if there was no parent to lay the egg in the first place.

Our one remaining hen, Owly, provides us with 3 or 4 eggs a week, when she's in the mood. When she's on strike or holiday, we buy organic free-range eggs from our neighbour, whose hens we know personally. Owly often visits to spend a couple of hours with them. They are a sociable little group, roaming around scratching here and there, pecking, murmuring amongst themselves, and shouting loudly when they have produced a perfect egg. They trundle happily around the fields, scratching, clucking and plucking up grass, insect delicacies and seeds, a completely natural diet that produces eggs as nature intended them to be. I don't know the nutritional value of commercially produced eggs, but I'm fairly sure that creatures kept in stacks of bare metal cages too small for them to stand up or turn around, showered with the faeces of those in the rows above them, fed on processed foods in buildings that are lit 24 hours a day so that they lay twice in 24 hours, cannot be laying eggs I want to eat.

With half a dozen eggs in the fridge, you always have a quick meal at hand. For comfort food, how much better does it get than a fried egg sandwich with a golden runny yolk surrounded by a glistening white with a crispy edge? Sublime.

Apart from being a miracle of design, an egg is packed full of goodness and versatility, but if you're entertaining it's a good idea to check with guests if they are allergic to eggs, and remember that raw eggs can be a source of salmonella, causing serious illness to the weak, very young, very old, and particularly to pregnant women.

In baking, apple purée or yoghurt make a good substitute for eggs. Replace each egg in the recipe with either ⅓ cup of apple purée, or ¼ cup of yoghurt. It works well in any dense-textured cake.

Fried egg with zing
What we call a fried egg the French call *oeuf sur le plat* – egg on the plate. I prefer mine on a slice of toast.

I think I make a good fried egg, cooking it over a moderate heat in melted butter, and flipping it over for Terry who prefers it cooked on both sides. However, a French friend who stayed with us showed me her way, which I have to say gives the dish an interesting twist and makes a change when you want something a little different from brown sauce or ketchup.

As soon as you have fried your egg and placed it on a slice of buttered toast, sprinkle a tablespoon of red wine vinegar or balsamic vinegar into the hot frying pan. Let is sizzle and evaporate for a moment and then pour it over the egg.

Chopped egg and onion
This simple dish is perfect for brunch, lunch or supper.

You need just four ingredients: hard-boiled eggs, spring onions, chives, and mayonnaise (see recipe under Sauces and Dressings).

Hard boil the eggs. When they are cool, chop them roughly and mix together with finely chopped spring onions (if you can't get spring onions, it works just as well with ordinary ones) chopped chives and mayonnaise, seasoning to taste with salt and pepper. That's it!
*Gluten free. *Raw egg**

Luxurious scrambled eggs
Here's a way to make simple scrambled eggs special. I learned it from a lady with a very loud voice and large bosoms, the chairwoman of a local fundraising charity, who frightened the wits out of me when I first met her and she invited us to dinner. I mentioned that we didn't eat meat, which she said would be no problem, she would make a fish pie.

28

*

There were four other guests, and the evening began rather uncomfortably, everything seemed very formal and even the most sociable man was failing to ignite us. We had a beautiful starter of smoked salmon, but as her husband cleared the table there was a shriek and a stream of unladylike language from the kitchen.

Our hostess had caught her skirt in the oven door as she pushed it closed with her knee while holding the hot fish pie. Off balance, she had slipped and dropped the pie. The floor was splattered with creamy sauce, pieces of fish, prawns and mashed potato. An elderly Labrador was trying to lick it up without burning its mouth.

We stood in the doorway, aghast. Then our hostess threw back her head, roared with laughter and herded us back into the dining room.

"Don't worry about the mess – Pluto will clear it up. Let's have another drink while we work out plan B."

The lady opposite me said, "How awful for you, Lorraine, I'm so sorry."

"Oh, it often happens. I'm as clumsy as a clown in the kitchen. Always dropping or burning things."

She pointed at me. "Come and give me a hand. We can get to know each other. Nathan – keep our guests topped up, there's a dear. "

I followed her into the kitchen where she wiped a mop over the floor which showed not a trace of fish pie thanks to the efforts of the dog.

"Have a look in the pantry and see how many eggs we have, will you?"

"20," I called back.

"Excellent, that'll do nicely. Let's get cracking!" She squeezed my shoulder and shook with laughter. "Nice pun, what!"

"What are we going to do with them?"

29

"We are going to make the best scrambled eggs ever," she chuckled. "You can start by chopping a couple of onions."

I chopped them very finely, while she melted a great chunk of butter in a giant frying pan. While the onions sizzled gently, we cracked the 20 eggs, one at a time into a glass (never risk cracking them into one another, because if you find a bad one, they're all ruined), and then beat them together with a fork.

As the onions became translucent she tipped the eggs in, and over a low heat stirred gently and continuously, while I prepared 8 thick slices of toast and popped it into the still-warm oven. As the eggs started to thicken, Lorraine poured in half a pint of double cream, a large pinch of salt and pepper, and stirred it all together.

I buttered the toast, and we finished the eggs with a couple of tablespoons of grated Parmesan. Once it was piled up on warmed plates, Lorraine snipped a few stalks of chives over the top of each slice.

"Tra-la-la," she chirruped, placing the plates in front of the guests.

Simple scrambled eggs transformed into a gourmet delight.

"Gorgeous," said one of the other guests, "absolutely splendid."

"Where did you find the recipe?" asked somebody else.

"No recipe, just made it up as I went along," Lorraine replied.

The room livened up immediately, with much laughter, and I thought how Lorraine had carried off a potential disaster with such aplomb, without letting her guests feel uncomfortable. And I learned that it was more important to let your guests relax than to feed them a complicated meal. I also saw that behind the façade of the accomplished hostess was somebody probably just as nervous as me.

Since then – and it was over 30 years ago – that's the way I nearly always serve scrambled eggs.

So to summarise: stir some finely chopped onion into some sizzling butter over a low heat until transparent, then add the beaten eggs and stir them until they start to thicken. Pour in a generous amount of cream, some salt and pepper, and continue cooking until the eggs are set. Then stir in some grated Parmesan and sprinkle with chopped chives. Serve on hot buttered toast.

Garlic poached eggs

This is strictly for lovers of garlic and will leave you with garlic breath for at least 24 hours. When we were working, we used to have it on Saturday or Sunday morning for breakfast. I confess I have never mastered the art of poaching eggs, other than in silicone moulds designed for the purpose. So if you have your own way of doing it, jolly good.

Take a whole unpeeled head of garlic – that's the whole thing, not one of the small segments. Peel off some of the loose outer skin but leave the bulb intact. Put it in a saucepan with plenty of boiling water, and simmer for about 15-20 minutes. Remove the garlic, but keep the water.

Mash the garlic with the blade of a knife - the papery covering should come off easily, leaving you with a creamy and mild-tasting garlic purée. Mix it well with plenty of butter.

Meanwhile poach the eggs in the water in which the garlic was simmered, and at the same time prepare a slice of toast for each egg.

Spread the garlic and butter mix on the warm toast, and top with the poached egg. Season well with salt. Think to yourself how wonderful life is.

Potato tortilla

Another dish that has numerous variations and is irresistible in all of them. This is how our Spanish friend Miguel cooked it for us, and it's our favourite. There are quicker recipes, but this one is worth the wait.

Allow one egg and two large potatoes per person, plus garlic according to taste. Peel the potatoes and cut them into walnut-sized pieces. Peel the garlic (place it on a board and whack it with the blade of a knife to peel off the papery skin) and chop it finely. Put the potato and garlic into a thick-bottomed pan with a generous helping of olive oil and a little salt, and let it cook over a very low heat until the potatoes are tender enough to mash – 40-50 minutes.

Pour off the oil and set it aside, and mash the potatoes and garlic into a smooth purée, adding more salt if necessary.

Now take a frying pan – either non-stick or cast iron – and pour in some of the left over olive oil. Get it really hot, then pour in the potato/egg mixture. Turn down the heat and let the tortilla cook gently until the top looks and feels fairly firm.

This is the tricky bit – take the pan from the heat, loosen the bottom of the tortilla, and slide it carefully onto a plate or chopping board. Don't do what I did – flip the raw side onto the plate and wonder why it all went wrong. Now put the pan over the tortilla and holding the plate or board firmly, lift it and tip the tortilla back into the pan, with the uncooked side face down. Continue cooking slowly until the tortilla is cooked through.

When Miguel makes this he turns it several times so that the tortilla doesn't burn, but does get cooked through thoroughly.

If like me you are not a proficient flipper, place the pan under a hot grill to finish cooking. Mind the hot handle when you take it out!
Gluten free

Eggy bread
This recipe takes me back to childhood holidays spent with a family who lived out in the African bush. There was no

electricity. Mpishi – the cook – whose kitchen was a primitive hut where he cooked on a stove heated by charcoal, made this for breakfast, bringing in a tray piled high, and every slice had vanished within seconds.

There are no specific quantities. You just beat some eggs well, with some milk in a shallow dish. Take some slightly stale bread slices (it will go all soggy if it's too fresh), and put them into the mixture, pushing under the mixture until they are well-coated all over. Fry the slices in butter in a frying pan over medium heat, turning once, so that both sides are golden brown.

We always ate it sprinkled with sugar and cinnamon, but you can eat it any way you like. A friend likes to place crispy fried bacon between two slices. She tells me it's the best breakfast ever.

Poor knights of Windsor
This takes eggy bread a stage further, into a treat my mother's friend Aunt Kitty used to make. Butter two slices of bread, and then spread them with a good layer of jam. Press the two slices firmly together. Crack an egg into a shallow dish, add a splash of milk, and dip the sandwiches in to cover both sides, pressing down well so that the bread absorbs a little of the mixture. Aunty Kitty deep fried them in lard. I shallow fry in butter over medium heat, turning once until both sides are golden brown. Sprinkle with a little sugar. Extreme comfort food.

5

Snacks, finger food and side dishes

Hummus

While we were staying at a villa on the island of Samos, the lady owner invited us to lunch and served a beautiful array of dishes. Her hummus was sensational. She showed me how she made it, saying that it was the traditional and authentic way. One can of chickpeas, drained; 2 tablespoons of olive oil; juice of one lemon; teaspoon of cumin powder; half a teaspoon of salt; pinch of black pepper; two cloves of garlic. She pounded it all together with a huge mortar and pestle until smooth, then spread it in a shallow dish, drizzled with more olive oil and garnished with a few black olives and some flat-leaf parsley. It was deliciously creamy, and didn't have that bitter undertone that tahini can give it.

I make it the same way – except I use a food processor. Sometimes I add a tablespoon of Greek yoghurt to make it extra creamy. You may want to experiment with the quantities of oil and juice to get the exact texture that you like.

The funny thing was that she had a ginger cat that loved hummus. It would sit and watch her intently as she pounded away with the mortar and pestle, and she always gave it a spoonful on a plate!
Vegan if you leave out the yoghurt, gluten free

Baba ganoush
Although it's Turkish in origin, it was on the menu in most restaurants when we used to holiday in the Greek islands. There are many different recipes, this is the one I use.

Put whole aubergines on a sheet of foil on a baking tray under a hot grill, prick them in a few places with a fork, and keep turning them until the skin is completely charred and the aubergine has collapsed. Leave them to cool, and then put them in a plastic bag until they are quite cold. Scrape out the pulp from the skin, and mash with a fork. Mix together into a thick paste with a tablespoon of olive oil per aubergine, two crushed cloves of garlic, a tablespoon of tahini, half a teaspoon of ground cumin, 1-2 tablespoons of fresh lemon juice, salt and parsley. Adjust to taste, and serve with pitta bread.
Vegan, gluten free without the pitta bread.

Skordalia
Here's another recipe that our Greek friend made for us, a powerful garlicky sauce that goes wonderfully well with fried fish or vegetables. I wouldn't have the energy to use a mortar and pestle as she did, but a food processor makes quick work of it. Skordalia keeps well in the fridge, so it's worth making loads.

Wash a heap of floury potatoes and boil them in their skins until tender. Immediately remove the skins and break the flesh up a little, putting it into the food processor while still hot with a handful of peeled garlic cloves, 1½ cups of olive oil, a teaspoon of salt and the juice of 4 lemons. Process into a smooth paste.
Vegan, gluten free

Apple and leek pastries
I found this recipe on a piece of paper at the bottom of an old handbag. No idea where or who it came from, and the directions are very sketchy, but it works well. You just have to work out the quantities for yourself!

Stew some cooking apples and finely sliced leeks in butter until tender. Drain off any liquid and stir in chopped sage and a little mustard.

Brush filo pastry with melted butter, layer three sheets on top of each other, cut into quarters, place a little of the apple/leek mixture on each, fold up into small parcels, and bake in a hot oven until crisp and golden.

Creamed mushrooms on toast
Finely slice mushrooms and cook them very slowly in a little melted butter with a clove of finely chopped garlic and a handful of parsley. When all the liquid has evaporated, season with salt and freshly ground black pepper and stir in a little double cream. Pile onto slices of hot buttered toast.

Crostini and bruschetta
The basis for crostini and bruschetta is toast, and the toppings are limited only by your imagination, savoury or sweet, in any combination you choose. What you must have, though, is proper toast. Not a bit of sliced loaf, but proper tasty toast made from a hearty rustic bread or slices of baguette. It's the difference between a small mouthful of stuff and a tasty titbit.

36

As a young child, before we went to live in Africa, our home was heated by a coal fire, and we toasted bread over the flames, on a long brass trident. The same method was used by my grandmother when I went to live with her. It produced the most flavoursome toast, slightly charred in parts, giving it that extra kick and flavour that an electric toaster doesn't accomplish.

When I was walking across France I met a lovely French lady called Laurence, who invited me to stay the night in her little cottage in the Auvergne. For breakfast, she cut thick slices of bread, heated a cast iron frying pan until it was too hot to touch, and dropped the bread onto it. Within a few seconds smoke was arising from around the bread, which she flicked over with a knife. The result was toast that was not quite burned, but flecked with small pieces of black, and it instantly transported me back to the days of the old coal fires, recalling memories of childhood, sitting in pyjamas and dressing gown and smelling the toast cooking, and then watching creamy butter sinking into it.

Ever since, I've used the dry frying pan method. It only works with cast iron. Don't put any fat in the pan. The pan needs to be very hot, and it only takes a few seconds for the toast to cook. Push the bread down with a spatula. You'll start to see wisps of smoke coming from the pan, then you know the toast is done. Then you have the basis for some good bruschetta.

At its simplest bruschetta is a piece of toast rubbed with the cut edge of a clove garlic, then topped with a smear of chopped tomatoes – fresh or tinned – drizzled with olive oil, sprinkled with salt and garnished with torn basil leaves. There isn't much difference between bruschetta and crostini. The latter are usually a little smaller, not quite as 'hearty' as bruschetta. Either make an ideal accompaniment to drinks with friends.

This recipe was given to me by a neighbour when we lived in Gloucestershire many moons ago – she always served it with Christmas morning drinks. Really delicious!

To 2 tablespoons of melted butter add 2 tablespoons of plain flour and cook over moderate heat for 1 minute, then slowly add 1 cup of milk, a little at a time, stirring all the time until the mixture boils. Remove from heat. Stir in 5 tablespoons of grated Parmesan cheese, 1 heaped cup of finely chopped mushrooms and 2 teaspoons of anchovy paste. Stir well. Spread the mixture on top of squares of toast, and bake in a hot oven for 5 minutes. Decorate each piece with a sliver of red pepper or half an olive.

Toppings are only limited by your imagination and the ingredients you have to hand. Have fun!

Cheese and asparagus fingers
This is one of the very rare occasions when I use commercial sliced bread, preferably wholemeal.

For four people, take 12 slices of bread and remove the crusts. Now roll the bread as thinly as you can with a rolling pin and cover with a clean damp cloth for about 15 minutes. Then spread the bread with a generous layer of Dijon mustard. In the middle put a slice of Emmental or Gruyere cheese the same length as the bread, and about 1" (2.5cm) wide. Place a spear of asparagus on top.

Carefully roll up the bread like a sausage roll, and secure with cocktail sticks. Brush the rolls with melted butter, and lay them on a buttered baking tray. Bake in a hot oven until golden brown, about 10-12 minutes and serve immediately.

Goats' cheese or feta, pear and walnut salad
Arrange a few green leaves – lambs lettuce or watercress work well – on a plate. Place on top a couple of slices of goats' cheese or feta. hop a couple of peeled, cored pears and sprinkle with lemon juice. Chop a handful of walnuts. Whisk together 2 tablespoons of olive oil and 1 tablespoon of lemon juice.

Top the cheese with nuts and pears, and dress with the oil and vinegar.
Gluten free

Smoked salmon squares
Lightly toast some sliced bread, and remove the crusts. Cut each slice into four small squares, and spread with cream cheese. Sprinkle with a little black pepper, and top with small pieces of smoked salmon, garnished with a fragment of fresh lemon. It also works well with garlic and herb cream cheese.

French style radishes
What to do with a radish is a puzzle I've worried about since the days of Aunt Ellen's fearsome salad. Unlike most other vegetables there doesn't seem to be anything you can actually do with it except eat it raw or carve it into a flower. It was my French friend Agnès who enlightened me when she served a radish starter. A plate of beautifully clean radishes with their tops left on to hold them with, a little heap of salt crystals, and a chunk of butter. You dip the radish into the butter, then into the salt. Simple. And delicious.
Gluten free

Stuffed dates
The first time we invited our French neighbours in for aperos, I served a selection of nibbles, and this was the firm favourite. They all loved the contrast between sweet and salty, and I heard one old lady say quietly to her friend: "Oh, I didn't think the food would be edible, but these are very good." :)

Split some nice fat dates and remove the stone. Stuff with a teaspoonful of soft blue cheese, or cream cheese sprinkled with a tiny amount of cayenne pepper.
Gluten free

Smoked fish pâté

My friend Abby kept house and was a live-in companion to an ancient rich harridan, I mean demanding, wealthy old lady, who kept her running around from the first note of birdsong in the morning until long after dark and didn't seem to ever need sleep. Luckily Abby had great stamina, not to mention the patience of Job and an uncrushably cheerful nature. Her duties had no limit, and no matter what else she had to do, food was to be served strictly on time. Three courses, twice daily. Abby had put together a large collection of recipes which enabled her to produce a meal at the click of a finger. Many of the recipes came from friends who worked for similarly wealthy people in stately homes, and they were surprising in their simplicity. This fish pâté was a great favourite with the old lady.

Remove any skin and stray bones from two fillets of smoked mackerel or trout, and mash them together with 2 tablespoons of soft butter, 2 tablespoons of double cream, a small onion, finely chopped, a finely chopped clove of garlic and a squeeze of lemon juice. Season to taste with salt and black pepper, and serve with toast. You can process instead of mashing, but I think mashing gives a better texture.

Melon and grape cocktail

A virtuous and elegant starter, ideal if you're going to follow with a heavy meal. Especially good on a hot summer day.

Mix together small cubes or balls of Cantaloupe or Honeydew melon with seedless grapes cut in half. Add plenty of finely chopped fresh mint, and dress with a mixture of 1 part cider vinegar to 4 parts of olive oil. Serve chilled.
Vegan, gluten free

Hush puppies

Quick and easy to make and cook, fluffy little balls of munchiness.

40

Mix 1 cup of fine cornmeal (polenta) with ½ tablespoon of plain flour, ¼ teaspoon of bicarbonate of soda, ½ teaspoon of salt. Add half a finely chopped onion, 1 beaten egg, and about half a cup of buttermilk (mix a teaspoon of lemon juice or vinegar into plain milk if you don't have any buttermilk.) Mix all the ingredients well. If the batter is too dry add a little more milk. Heat some vegetable (not olive) oil. I use a small, cheap wok as I didn't get on very well with the deep fat fryer; it was always sticky and a bit smelly. Heat the oil until a drop of the batter rises to the surface within 10 seconds. You don't want the oil to be smoking, just hot. Fry dessertspoons of the mixture for about 2 minutes on each side, until they are floating and golden. Drain on kitchen paper, and serve straight away.
Vegan, gluten free

Peppers and feta
Cheese and vinegar sounds like an unlikely marriage, but this recipe is really flavoursome and works well.

Thinly slice some red peppers. Fry them in a couple of tablespoons of olive oil over medium heat until they soften and turn floppy. Add a clove or two of very finely chopped garlic and stir around for a few seconds to let the garlic cook, but not brown.

Remove the pan from the heat, and sprinkle with a tablespoon of Balsamic vinegar, a tablespoon of capers, and a cup of cubed Feta cheese. Serve at room temperature.
Gluten free

Welsh rabbit
When grated cheese on toast just won't do, go a step further and jazz it up into Welsh Rabbit.

Four four people, be generous with the cheese – use about 1 lb. (0.45kg) of good strong cheese like Cheddar. Grate it and put it in a saucepan with two tablespoons of butter and let it melt slowly. Add ¼ cup of ale and a good teaspoon of mustard. Stir constantly until the mixture is thick and creamy.

Beat a couple of egg yolks with another ¼ cup of ale, and stir into the mixture until it's smooth.

Heap it onto hot toast, close your eyes and inhale it for a few seconds before taking your first heavenly mouthful.

6

A Few Words About Miracle Foods

Surely I'm not the only person who has been completely baffled by the pronouncements of nutritionists and dietitians? One will tell you that grains and legumes are essential to good health; another will say they should be cut out of your diet completely. Broccoli is good for you, unless you have a thyroid condition in which case it's bad for you. Animal fat is good. Animal fat is bad. Carbohydrate is bad. Carbohydrate is essential. You should eat an egg every day. You should only eat 2 eggs a week. It goes on and on, leaving you wondering what on earth you can and should eat.

Every month a new 'wonder' food is heralded – not a cheap, readily available fruit or vegetable like a carrot or cucumber, but an astonishingly expensive berry or oil or powder. Bilberries, açai berries, maqui berries, cranberries, blueberries, baobab powder, detoxifiers, weight loss aids, anti-oxidants, anti-carcinogenics, age reversing – REALLY? There is, it seems, nothing these ingredients can't achieve for your health, up to and including eternal youth and eternal life. There's a reason it's called the health food industry! With the emphasis on 'industry'.

When did that all begin? When I was growing up food was something you had two or three times a day, which the body needed to grow, something eaten with pleasure (usually), everything eaten in moderation. There was no 'bad' food and no 'magic' food. Some things tasted better than others. Chocolate was tastier than spinach, but you had to eat smaller amounts. In any case, in those years following WWII, there

43

wasn't that much chocolate to be had. And when we did, one bar was broken into small pieces, one tablet per person. The rest was carefully wrapped up and put away for the next day. So a bar could last 3 or 4 days. Now it's common to eat a whole bar in one go – I know – I've done that often enough.

We knew that if you ate too much, you would get fat, and in you didn't eat enough you would be underweight and if you ate too much sugar you'd have bad teeth. I believe the nearest you can get to a 'miracle' for good health and healthy weight is to eat quality, fresh ingredients, in moderation and as little processed food as possible. If anybody ever should discover a magical foodstuff that is proven beyond doubt to prevent and cure all diseases, keep everybody forever young and beautiful, then I'll be rushing to buy it. In the meantime, I just try to feed my family and friends well using natural ingredients.

7

Soups

Soups have everything going for them. They're inexpensive, nutritious, very quick and easy to prepare, perfect for busy or lazy cooks. They're easy to eat – either at table from a bowl with a spoon, sitting around the fire sipping from a mug or chilled in a flask for an al fresco summer meal. I make them in huge quantities and freeze them. Unfortunately I usually forget to label them or think I'll remember what they are so I rarely know what we're going to be eating.

They can be light and elegant starters, or hearty complete meals in themselves.

I don't like watery soups. It probably dates back to the time before I stopped eating meat, when I tried to make a genuine beef consommé. It took hours, roasting the bones and vegetables, then boiling them to make the stock and straining it several times. After about six hours it was time for the final step, adding beaten egg white to clear the soup and give it a beautiful transparency. I tipped the beaten egg into the mixture, and then strained it for the final time. Straight down the kitchen sink.

As a small child I had great difficulty in swallowing food. I could chew jelly and ice-cream for hours, much to the despair of my mother, particularly when I had to stay in bed in a darkened room for nearly a month, first with measles and immediately afterwards with German measles. My throat was very sore, which, added to the problem of swallowing my food, meant everything she tried to feed me churned around and around in my mouth as I fought to gulp it down and drove her to tears of frustration. It was bad enough when I was fit and well, but now I was an invalid she had to get food into me somehow.

One lunchtime she placed a tray in front of me. On it was a fragrant dish containing a small mountain of soft, buttery perfectly mashed potato, surrounded by an ocean of Heinz Cream of Tomato Soup.

"It's a volcano," she said, "popping up out of the sea. The sea is red because of the lava coming out of the volcano." We'd recently read a story about volcanoes.

It was delicious, comforting and relatively easy for me to swallow. I stirred the potato around in the soup until it amalgamated into one orange-tinted glistening mess, and I cleaned the plate.

Generally I don't like soup from tins or cartons, because I can always discern a slightly metallic taste, but I can't resist Heinz Cream of Tomato, which takes me back to childhood in that darkened bedroom, watching the steam rising and inhaling the aroma. With an added portion of mashed potato, and a knob of butter.

Vichyssoise
An elegant and sophisticated classic French soup that is served chilled. A reminder of the evening we invited friends for dinner, and during aperitifs the conversation revolved around food. One of our guests announced that he ate anything and everything, except cold soup which he loathed. As I had already prepared Vichyssoise, I said I would heat his for him, but he said he would try it cold. He did eat it all and said that it was delicious. So it's worth checking beforehand with guests if you plan on serving a chilled soup.

To serve four, peel and dice 4 large floury potatoes and finely slice 1 medium leek, including the green part. Put them in a large saucepan with a cup of fresh or frozen peas and a knob of butter, and stir over low heat for 2-3 minutes, until the vegetables are well-coated with the butter.

Add 1½ cups of boiling stock and simmer until the vegetables are tender, about 15 minutes. Cool thoroughly, and then blend to a smooth purée. You can push the vegetables through a strainer if you don't have an electric liquidiser or hand blender.

NEVER try to liquidise very hot mixtures – they will expand, force their way out of the lid of the liquidiser, spit and splatter all over the place, and burn you.

Season to taste, then stir in 1 cup of double cream. Chill well, and sprinkle with chopped chives to serve. Add some chive flowers too if you have them; they look very pretty on this pastel-green soup, and are edible.
Gluten free

Strawberry soup
The Sun King in all his splendour, Louis XIV, apparently loved this soup. So do we, although some guests may find a chilled fruit soup strange, so if you know they are picky eaters, it may

not be right for them. This recipe is particularly fresh and tasty, without any dairy products in it.

Mix a cup of dry white wine with ⅓ cup of sugar, and bring to the boil. Add 3 cups of chopped strawberries - buy them when they're in season and full of flavour. Forced strawberries don't have a rich enough flavour to do this soup justice. Leave to simmer for 5 minutes, then remove from the heat.

Push the mixture through a sieve to produce a thick purée. You can process it but I prefer to sieve because it removes the seeds and results in a smoother purée.

Stir in one cup of pure orange juice, and refrigerate until quite cold. Serve garnished with a teaspoon of finely chopped fresh mint.
Vegan, gluten free

Gazpacho version 1
The healthiest soup imaginable – a rich liquid salad. It has existed in Spain for centuries and there are countless recipes for it. Originally it was made by very finely chopping, pounding and/or sieving the vegetables. Thanks to the electric blender or liquidiser, it's far quicker and easier to make now.

This is the recipe I've been using for 40 years, and the following should serve at least 6 people.

1 clove of garlic
6 large ripe tomatoes, chopped
1 Spanish onion, chopped
1 green pepper, chopped
1 cucumber, peeled and chopped
4 tablespoons of lemon juice
6 tablespoons of olive oil
2 cups of tomato juice
salt and cayenne pepper

Process all the ingredients, in small batches, to a thick purée. Chill thoroughly to serve.

I like it just like that, but it can be accompanied by fresh bread crumbs, with side helpings of chopped raw onion, chopped hard-boiled egg, chopped tomato, and ice cubes.
Vegan, gluten free without breadcrumbs

Gazpacho version 2
Our Spanish friend Miguel's family recipe is simpler than mine, with less ingredients, and tastes just as good. You have free rein here as to the quantities of vegetables you use and how many you are catering for! Make sure there are plenty of really ripe red tomatoes, though.

Nice red ripe tomatoes, chopped
Garlic, crushed
Cucumber, peeled and chopped
Sweet red pepper, chopped
Water
Olive oil
Salt
Balsamic vinegar

Put all the vegetables into a large bowl. Blend them a few at a time with water, olive oil and vinegar until fairly smooth. Repeat until it is all blended. Season to taste, then refrigerate.

You can add a lot of water to this soup, without it losing its flavour. Either dilute it with cold water, or serve with ice cubes.
Gluten free, vegan

Carrot and orange soup
A sunny golden soup with a nice fresh taste. Peel and slice 5-6 large carrots, and put in a saucepan with a chunk of butter, 2 cloves of garlic, a pinch of saffron, a tablespoon of sugar and half a teaspoon of ground ginger, or fresh grated ginger. Stew

gently in the butter for 6-8 minutes. Add the juice of 4 large oranges and 4 cups of water, bring to the boil and simmer for 45 minutes. Allow to cool, then blend to a smooth purée. Season to taste and reheat to serve, garnished with grated orange rind and a swirl of cream or yoghurt.
Gluten free

Cream of onion soup
French onion soup really only works if it's based on a strong beef stock, and as a non-meat eater that puts it out of my orbit. I have tried with various vegetable stocks but the result was watery and insipid. Instead I prefer this lovely, thick creamy onion soup, a recipe given to me by my friend Liz.

To serve four people, chop 4 large onions and 4 medium potatoes into dice of about 3/4".

Melt a large knob of butter over a gentle heat, and stew the vegetables with the lid on, until the onions just begin to turn golden, and the potatoes are tender, about 20 minutes, checking every few minutes to make sure the vegetables aren't sticking. Add 4-5 cups of hot stock and continue cooking for another 10 minutes.

Allow to cool, then blend to a thick purée. Stir in one cup of single cream and a pinch of nutmeg, season to taste, and reheat to serve.
Gluten free

Roasted sweet potato and garlic soup
Peel and chop 4 large sweet potatoes and 1 large onion and put them in a roasting tin. Add 20 cloves of peeled garlic and drench with ¼ cup of olive oil. Bake at 200C for about 20 minutes, until the vegetables are tender.

Now tip them into a large saucepan with 6 cups of vegetable stock, and bring up to the boil. Take off the heat and leave to

50

cool, then blend or liquidise into a creamy purée. Stir in ½ cup of cream cheese and season to taste.

Reheat to serve, garnishing with freshly-chopped chives.
Gluten free

Pea souper soup
The notorious smog – a mixture of fog and coal fire smoke – that choked the London air up to and during the 1950s was known as a 'pea souper' because it was so thick you could almost chew it. Boarding school food was very varied – from inedible-unless-you-were-famished to just about edible; except for the green pea soup, which was indescribably delicious, so thick that your spoon could stand upright in it without support. The stock was based on ham bone. I use a vegetable stock and find the taste is just as good.

Chop a large onion fairly finely, and let it sizzle gently in a knob or butter, or glug of oil until the onion begins to turn golden at the edges. Toss in a cupful of green split peas, 2 teaspoons of crushed coriander seeds (I use a coffee grinder), and 2 crushed cloves of garlic and stir for 30 seconds – don't let the garlic burn. Add 6 cups of boiling stock, a couple of bay leaves, salt and pepper, cover and cook for an hour or until the peas have softened completely into a mush. Give it a splash of milk. Remove the bay leaves before serving. You can blend it into a smooth mixture, or leave it a little lumpy, and the coriander seeds will add a little texture.

Crispy croutons make a good addition to this warming soup. And a drizzle of truffle oil makes it extra special.
Omit croutons for gluten free version. For vegans, use oil instead of butter, and omit milk.

Butternut squash soup
Half an hour from start to finish for a glorious velvety golden bowl of loveliness. What more could you ask? Honestly, this is just divine.

Note: I watched somebody trying to peel a butternut squash with a potato peeler. What a struggle! It's far easier to cut the squash into round slices about 1" thick, and just cut away the skin with a sharp knife.

Slice a couple of onions and pop them in a large saucepan with a generous knob of butter. Let them melt over a very gentle heat for about 10 minutes, until they are soft and transparent, but not coloured. Throw in chunks of 1 large or 2 medium peeled butternut squash – and a couple of cooking apples, peeled, cored and chopped. Stir them around to coat in the butter, keeping the heat low, and then put the lid on. Leave them to enjoy the buttery steam for another 10 minutes, and then add 4-5 cups of boiling stock. Simmer for another 10 minutes, by which time the squash should be very tender. Remove from the heat, and purée with a blender. (Remember not to put very hot liquid in a liquidiser – it will erupt and scald you and decorate your kitchen.) Check the seasoning. There, it's ready. There is nothing to stop you adding a tablespoon of cream cheese if you feel like gilding the lily, but personally I think it doesn't need more than a sprinkle of parsley.
Gluten free. *Replace the butter with oil and omit cream cheese for a vegan version*

Creamy lentil soup
Comfort in a cup.

Crush 2 teaspoons of coriander seeds, then stir for a couple of minutes in a knob of melted butter or tablespoon of oil. Add one cup of lentils, two crushed cloves of garlic and 6 cups of hot stock.

Simmer until the lentils are tender, about 40 minutes, then add a cup of milk and a handful of fresh breadcrumbs. Bring back to the boil for 5 minutes. Season to taste, and whizz with a hand blender. For a velvety finish, push through a fine mesh strainer.
Omit breadcrumbs for a gluten free version

Cream of mushroom soup
Sauté a medium chopped onion, a large diced potato and 4 cups of sliced mushrooms in butter for 5 minutes or until all the liquid from the mushrooms has evaporated. Add 4 cups of boiling stock and simmer for 20-30 minutes then allow to cool. Blend to a smooth purée, add 2 tablespoons of cream, season with salt and pepper, and garnish with freshly chopped thyme or tarragon.
Gluten free

That lovely green soup you made once
I make lots of soups, in varying shades of green. So when my husband asked if I'd make "that lovely green soup you made once," I asked if he could be more specific. Was it the spinach soup? No, it definitely wasn't spinach. Vichyssoise, perhaps? No, it was hot. What shade of green, I asked? A sort of nice bright green, like a spring leaf. Was it hot and spicy? No, it was just tasty. Really fresh and nice. "How long ago did we have it?" I asked. He thought it was when those people came for lunch. "Which people?" Those people whose names he couldn't remember. But they were friends of friends. A few years ago.

I spent nearly two days going through piles of my recipes trying to find the nice leaf-green soup. This is it – pea and lettuce. :) 30 minutes from start to finish.

Sauté a chopped shallot or small onion in a knob of butter until the onion is soft, about 5 minutes. Add 1 clove of chopped garlic, 2 teaspoons of sugar, ½ teaspoon of salt, 3 cups of fresh or frozen peas, one lettuce, shredded, and 4 cups of stock. Bring to the boil then simmer for 10-15 minutes, until peas are tender. Cool slightly, then blend into a smooth purée. You can add a swirl of single cream and a sprinkle of chopped mint if you like, but the soup tastes good without them. It can be served hot, but is also good chilled.

Vegan if you replace the butter with olive oil and omit the cream; gluten-free

Parsnip and apple soup

Stew 6 medium parsnips, peeled and chopped, and 1 sharp cooking apple, peeled, cored and chopped, in a large knob of butter for 10 minutes, stirring from time to time. Add 4 sage leaves, 2 cloves and 5 cups of stock. Simmer until parsnip is softened, about 30 minutes. Remove sage leaves and cloves and allow to cool. Process into a creamy purée. Season to taste. To serve, reheat, add a dollop of cream, and garnish with parsley or croutons.

Gluten free - omit croutons

Cider soup

We had this at a friend's house one bitterly cold winter night when their electricity suddenly went off. Luckily they had a gas hob and a log fire, and we sat around the flames, with candles burning, and drank gallons of this soup. The mixture of the flames, the smell of wood smoke, and the quantity of alcohol in the soup meant that we all ended up asleep in our chairs. Probably we shouldn't have driven home afterwards.

Bring to the boil 8 cups of dry cider, and stir in ½ cup of brown sugar.

Beat 3 eggs with 2 tablespoons of sugar, 1 ½ cups of cream, 2 tablespoons of flour, a pinch of allspice and 3 tablespoons of rum.

Whisk into the cider until it comes back to the boil. Serve immediately. It should have been served with cheese croutons, but we had it with chunks of baguette, soaking up every last drop. Guaranteed to warm you up on the very coldest night.
Not suitable for teetotallers

Zanzibari fish soup
This is a delicious and substantial fish soup that makes a good lunch or supper dish with some crusty bread.

Cut 2 lbs. (1 kilo) of firm white fish into 1" (2.5cm) cubes. Finely chop 4 sticks of celery, 2 leeks and 2 large onions and fry in ¼ cup of oil for 3-4 minutes, then add 2 teaspoons of curry powder, two cloves of finely chopped garlic, half a teaspoon of salt and 1 small green chilli, finely chopped. Stir for 1 minute, then add 8 cups of stock and 1-1½ cups of coconut cream. Stir well, then add 8 large peeled and chopped tomatoes. Cook over a moderate heat for 10 minutes, then add a large handful of chopped fresh coriander (cilantro) and half a cup of freshly squeezed lime juice. Continue cooking for 1-2 minutes, then serve immediately.
Gluten free

Curried apple soup
Another of Abby's swift recipes – half an hour from start to serve.

Finely chop one onion and fry gently in 1 tablespoon of butter until transparent. Stir in 2 tablespoons of flour and 1 tablespoon of medium curry powder, stir for a minute or so then add 3 cups of stock, 6 large cooking apples peeled, cored and chopped, and the juice of half a lemon.

Simmer until the apples are tender – about 10-15 minutes. Allow to cool for a few minutes, season with salt and pepper, then blend until smooth. Stir in ¼ pint of single cream and reheat just before serving.

Cream of green pea soup

Soften a chopped onion in a couple of tablespoons of butter over a moderate heat for 10 minutes. Add 4 cups of boiling stock and a large potato roughly chopped. Simmer until the potato is tender, and then add 2 cups of frozen peas. Continue simmering until peas are tender - 8-10 minutes. Cool slightly, then add a heaped tablespoon of chopped fresh mint, and blend to a smooth purée. Add two tablespoons of cream, or creamy milk. Season to taste, and serve hot or cold, garnished with extra freshly chopped mint.
Gluten free

A few words about Parmesan

Whenever possible I prefer to buy Parmesan cheese in a chunk rather than grated. The trouble is that I have such a passion for it that I can't resist breaking off pieces and eating them, so by the time I get home it's nearly all gone. If you have a left over Parmesan crust, save it until you are making a vegetable soup, and toss it in during cooking to let the flavour seep into the soup.

Fewer Words About Minestrone

I haven't been able to eat minestrone soup since the infamous 'sick bag' sketch by Barry Humphries.

8

Main Courses

PASTA

Once you had eaten my Italian mother-in-law's cooking, you would find it difficult to appreciate any Italian restaurant food. It wasn't about lashings of tomato sauce and a prancing waiter with a giant peppermill and Parmesan grater. Mamma could take a handful of herbs, a clove of garlic, some oil and butter and a smidgin of meat, a splash of Marsala, and create flavours that would make any food critic swoon. She didn't use dozens of ingredients, just a few, well-chosen. Her raison d'étre was to cook. Her tiny apartment was strewn with soft, silky pasta draped over the backs of chairs and the ironing board; ravioli and tortellini on trays on the bed. Everywhere you looked, there was pasta, and from the kitchen always aromas that flooded your mouth with saliva. You thought you had died and gone to heaven.

Being so quick to cook, it's a perfect meal for entertaining when you don't have a lot of time to spare.

When cooking pasta, it's best drained when still al dente, with a small amount of the cooking water retained. The pasta continues to absorb this and will not stick.

Mamma's Italian tomato sauce

This was my mother-in-law's recipe, and she was without question the best Italian cook. She handmade all her pasta, never used a dried herb or frozen vegetable, and when she wasn't in church she was in the kitchen preparing the next meal. Her little apartment was an Aladdin's cave of heavenly aromas, and even in the best Italian restaurants I haven't eaten food that tasted as good as Mamma's.

1 kg of ripe plum tomatoes. You can substitute drained tinned tomatoes if fresh aren't available.
2 cloves of garlic, very finely chopped
Half an onion, very finely chopped
Half a small carrot, very finely chopped
Half a stick of celery, very finely chopped
½ tablespoon chopped parsley
⅓ cup of olive oil
1 tablespoon caster sugar

If using fresh tomatoes, skin them by plunging in boiling water for 10 seconds. Then chop into quarters. Gently fry the chopped vegetables, garlic and parsley in the olive oil until the onion is soft, then add the chopped tomatoes, the sugar, a generous pinch of salt, a little ground black pepper. Cook, covered, over a very low heat until the sauce is thick. The longer the cooking time, the richer the flavour.
Vegan, gluten free

Mushroom and cream sauce
To prepare the mushroom sauce, fry 2 cups of chopped mushrooms gently in a mixture of 2 tablespoons of butter and 2 tablespoons of olive oil, with two cloves of crushed garlic and a handful of finely chopped parsley. Cook very slowly until the mushrooms are tender and there is no liquid remaining. Stir in ½ pt (280ml) single cream and a pinch of salt. Reheat gently and serve immediately with plenty of grated Parmesan cheese and black pepper.
Gluten free

No meat spaghetti carbonara
Mamma made a glorious carbonara sauce. I substitute smoked salmon pieces for the bacon and it's just as good.

Fry one finely sliced onion and 1 cup of diced smoked salmon in a tablespoon of butter, until golden brown. Pour in 1 wineglass of white wine and cook over moderate heat until almost evaporated.

Whisk together 3 eggs and ¼ cup of grated Parmesan cheese, 1 heaped tablespoon of chopped parsley and a grinding of black pepper. Cook spaghetti, drain quickly, return to the pan and add a knob of butter. Pour in the egg mixture, stir around for a minute to allow the egg to cook, then add the onion and smoked salmon. Serve immediately.

Alfredo sauce
This most indulgent of all the pasta sauces is pure fat so best eaten sparingly and seldom. :)

Stir together ⅓ of a cup of butter and ⅔ cup double cream over gentle heat until the butter has melted. Add ½ cup of freshly-grated Parmesan cheese, stir well, season with salt and pepper and serve immediately, sprinkled with a little chopped parsley.
Gluten free

Hot-pants sauce

It's more usually known as puttanesca sauce – meaning hookers' sauce, but we always called it hot-pants sauce because the ladies of the night would stand beside the road next to their little braziers, advertising their wares in the tiniest hot-pants.

It's a really gutsy sauce with a huge flavour – guaranteed to warm the coldest heart on a cold evening with a glass or two of rich red wine.

Mash 6 anchovy fillets, a large clove of garlic and a tablespoon of finely grated lemon zest into a thick paste. Fry 4 tablespoons of drained capers in ¼ cup of olive oil until the capers turn brown and begin to shrivel, then add the mashed mixture with ½ cup of chopped parsley, 2 tablespoons of lemon juice, ½ a teaspoon of dried red peppers and half a dozen chopped black olives. Serve with freshly cooked pasta and plenty of grated Parmesan.
Gluten free

Spaghetti with olive oil and garlic

Pasta at its simplest. Cook your pasta in plenty of boiling salted water. While it's cooking, gently fry a couple of cloves of very finely chopped garlic in a couple of tablespoons of olive oil or olive oil and butter, without letting the garlic brown. Drain the pasta, stir in the garlic and oil, add a good twist of freshly-ground black pepper, a tablespoon of chopped parsley and a generous helping of Parmesan cheese. That's all.

RISOTTO

Northern Italy is the home of risotto, where the rice grows abundantly in the Po valley. Forget long grain, Basmati, or any of the fancy rices. Risotto rice must be one of the round varieties, ideally Carnaroli or Arborio. The essential thing is that it is normal round rice, and not quick-cooking, because good risotto needs time to cook.

Baked risotto

This is my adaptation of a recipe which came with my Kenwood Chef in 1968, and has followed us around the world ever since. However, it is not a traditional Italian risotto cooked on the stove top, but is baked in the oven, so it breaks the 'round rice' rule and uses long grain instead.

Sauté a small, finely chopped onion and a crushed clove of garlic in a tablespoon of butter until transparent. Add 2 cups of long grain rice and stir for a few moments. Add ¾ cup of chopped mushrooms, 1 cup of chopped tomatoes, a pinch of saffron (or turmeric), and 1½ cups of stock. Bring up to the boil stirring. Check seasoning. Turn into an oven-proof dish and stir in ⅓ cup of grated Cheddar cheese. Cover, and cook in a moderate oven- 190C/375F until the rice is tender, about 25 minutes.
Gluten free

Mushroom risotto

As made by my Italian mother-in-law.

Crush two cloves of garlic and fry in 2 tablespoons of olive oil and 2 tablespoons of butter until the garlic just begins to turn golden. Remove the garlic and throw it away. Fry 3 cups of finely chopped mushrooms gently in the oil and butter until very soft and all the liquid has evaporated. Add half a cup of milk and a tablespoon of chopped parsley, continue cooking until the milk has evaporated and the mushrooms are soft and creamy.

Meanwhile cook round rice in stock until tender. Stir in the mushrooms and serve immediately with plenty of Parmesan cheese.
Gluten free

Cauliflower and sultana risotto

This is a mild tasting and unusual risotto. It is a recipe that my stepmother made. Our relationship was a very difficult one; she was a strange woman who resented and was never able to accept that she was a second wife, and I was a constant reminder of the fact. She brought much grief into my life, and the only good memories I have are of her cooking, which was excellent, even though meals were strained and often eaten in uncomfortable silence. Still, our lives are made up of memories both good and bad.

For four people you need to chop some cauliflower – about half a large one – into fairly small pieces, including the stalk and some of the smaller green leaves.

Melt a mixture of olive oil and butter in a large pan and stir in some finely chopped onion – about half an onion – a clove of crushed garlic, a cup of round rice, and the chopped cauliflower. Stir around in the fat until everything is coated, and then add a cup of stock. Bring to the boil and lower the heat so that the risotto cooks very slowly. Keep adding boiling stock as the rice absorbs it. When the rice is almost cooked, toss in a handful of sultanas or raisins, a knob of butter and a plentiful grating of Parmesan or Cheddar cheese. Season well with salt and ground black pepper. Turn off the heat, cover with a lid, and leave to stand for 5 minutes. Check the seasoning and serve immediately, adding a little chopped parsley and more Parmesan.

Gluten free

Gorgonzola risotto

We used to go skiing every winter, generally to Italy because they have the best food. :)

I hated the actual skiing part. I'm hopeless, always falling over and twisting things, or getting hooked on the chairlift by my jacket and making an exhibition of myself. But as a spectator sport, sitting in the sun on top of a mountain with a cup of coffee, it takes some beating. The huts at the top of the mountains served hearty, simple peasant foods at lunchtime, generally either a risotto or a polenta dish. One hut did the most amazing Gorgonzola risotto. I asked for the recipe, and was given some very basic details. Here's the result.

Sauté a finely chopped onion in 2 tablespoons of oil until transparent. Add ¾ of a cup of risotto rice and stir for a couple of minutes to coat the rice, then add ½ a wine glass of dry white wine. Let it sizzle until it has evaporated, then add boiling stock, a cup at a time, and simmer gently, stirring every few minutes, until the rice is just tender, adding more stock as necessary.

Meantime mash together ½ a cup of Gorgonzola cheese and 2 tablespoons of single cream. As soon as the rice is cooked stir in the cheese mixture and cover with a cloth and saucepan lid for 5 minutes to allow the flavours to develop. Serve with a good grinding of black pepper and grated Parmesan cheese.
Gluten free

Risotto Milanese
This is a simple dish that needs careful cooking, and reminds me of an embarrassing hostessing evening.

The traditional recipe includes bone marrow and chicken stock. This one doesn't, but it still tastes every bit as good as the one my mother-in-law used to make. It's rich, creamy and golden in colour.

I had an unfortunate experience with it when I invited friends to dinner. They all loved Italian food, and I served the Venetian sole recipe as a starter with some mixed antipasto, and the risotto as a main course. When I put it on the table the guests all sat looking at it in silence, waiting for something else to arrive. I served them and asked them to start eating. They looked nervously at each other, seeming to think I had forgotten something. Vegetables maybe? Anyway they all ate it and took second helpings, but nobody spoke. Not a single word through all two helpings. I was certain they couldn't believe all they were getting to eat was a heap of rice, no matter how beautifully it was made. When their plates were empty I put the salad and cheeseboard on the table, and they all began talking again. We ended the meal with a beautiful dessert – the raspberry Malakoff. It was a good evening, but there was a strange pall hanging over us, as if our friends were still certain there should have been something else with the rice, but they were too polite to mention it.

For six people, chop a medium sized onion finely, and fry in a tablespoon of butter until soft and golden. Stir in 2 cups of round rice, keep stirring until it begins to turn translucent, and then splash in a wine glass of dry white wine. Inhale that delicious aroma, still stirring as the wine evaporates.

You need to have 4 - 5 cups of boiling stock to hand. Keep adding it to the rice in cupfuls, over a moderate heat, stirring to prevent sticking, adding more when the liquid has almost evaporated. When the rice is almost done – keep testing it every few minutes – add a pinch of saffron dissolved in a tablespoon of stock – which will give it a soft golden colour. Stir in a tablespoon of butter, 2 tablespoons of grated Parmesan, a tablespoon of chopped parsley, and season well.
Gluten free

PIES AND TARTS

Pastry – it's a piece of pie!
There's always been something of a mystique about pastry-making, as if it's beyond the ability of mere mortals, requiring chilled marble work surfaces, iced water, frozen fingers lighter than a fairy's kiss.

Well, I have to admit I haven't attempted flaky pastry, or strudel pastry, because as you know, I don't have much patience. However, I can produce some pretty decent pie crust and tart bases without even getting it under my fingernails. Do you ever find that when you're hands are covered in dough either the phone rings, or your nose itches? Well, with these pastry recipes, that won't be a problem.

Rich, light shortcrust pastry
This gives a really light shortcrust pastry, and is easy to make if you have a food processor.
1½ cups of soft butter (you can substitute margarine)
4 cups of plain flour
Pinch of salt
3-4 tablespoons cold water

In a food processor cream together the water, butter and 4 tablespoons of the flour. Add the remaining flour a little at a time until you have a dough. Knead very gently into a ball, and chill for 30 minutes before using.

Hot water pastry
Put in a mixing bowl 1½ cups of plain flour, a pinch of salt and a pinch of baking powder. Pour over ½ cup of oil (not olive), and ¼ cup of boiling water. Mix it with a knife or spoon. It's going to look very runny, but don't panic! Keep mixing for a minute or so, when it will come together into a manageable dough as it begins to cool. Wrap it in clingfilm and put in the fridge to chill for an hour before use. Makes one 8" pie. This is quite a sticky pastry, best rolled out between two sheets of greaseproof paper, and used as a tart base. It is very short and crumbly, and according to my husband, the best pastry he's ever tasted. And he's a bit of a pastry fan.
Vegan

Stirred pastry
Crazily easy to make, and lower in fat than the rich light shortcrust.

Put in a mixing bowl 2 scant cups of plain flour, 1 teaspoon of salt, 1 teaspoon of sugar. Pour over ½ cup of oil (not olive) and ¼ cup of milk. Stir until you can't see any flour. Pat into a ball and chill for half an hour. Don't leave it too long before using, as it quickly becomes oily. A good strong pastry for pasties and pies. Makes sufficient for two 10" tarts or one pie.
Use soya milk for vegan version

Pissaladière
France's riposte to pizza. A pastry crust smothered with caramelised onions, decorated with black olives and anchovies. If cooking for vegans or strict vegetarians, omit the anchovies. If you don't like olives, leave them off. You will still be left with an exquisite onion-delight.

Finely slice 6-8 medium onions. Put them in a heavy pan over the lowest possible heat, with a large knob of butter or a couple of tablespoons of olive oil and a handful of fresh thyme leaves. Leave them to luxuriate in the fat for about an hour, while you make the pastry base. By then they should be mellow and golden. Stir in a tablespoon of sugar and continue cooking for a couple of minutes. Season with salt and pepper.

Roll out your pastry (the stirred pastry recipe works well) into a circle or rectangle. Pile on the onions and spread them evenly over the pastry. Traditionally anchovy fillets are laid over the top of the onions in a lattice, with a black olive in each square. Bake at 200C/425F for 25-30 minutes. Serve at room temperature, drizzled with a little olive oil and some fresh thyme.
Use oil for a vegan version

Garlic and pine nut tartlets
Very rich, very garlicky, very delicious. Very easy.

The filling: Toast 2 tablespoons of pine nuts under a moderate grill, or in a frying pan, for a couple of minutes until they just begin to turn golden. Whip them off the heat quickly otherwise they will continue to cook and burn. Process into a rough paste 8 tablespoons of butter, 5 cloves of garlic, 2 heaped teaspoons of fresh marjoram or oregano, a pinch of salt and pepper, half a cup of fresh breadcrumbs and the toasted pine nuts. Divide the mixture between 4 tartlet tins lined with hot water pastry and bake at 200C/425F for 10-15 minutes, until golden brown. Garnish with half a black olive and a sprig of fresh oregano, and serve warm.

Goat cheese and mint tart

This recipe was given to me by a friend of a friend, himself a non-meat eater. It has since become a favourite with our guests, who often ask if we'll be having what one of my beautiful granddaughters, Catherine, calls 'the green pie'.

It is so easy and obliging, and guaranteed to succeed provided you bear in mind one vital fact: mint jelly is not the same as mint sauce. Mint sauce is vinegary and liquid; mint jelly is thicker, sweeter and jelly-like, as the name implies. If you get it wrong, you'll have a horrible disaster.

So, you need sufficient pastry to line a flan dish. Use ready-made shortcrust pastry, or the hot water crust pastry recipe.

Now take a roll of goat's cheese and a jar of mint jelly. Mash them together roughly, or mix them in a food processor. It doesn't matter which. Add an egg, if you like, or two. It doesn't matter if you don't add any. The eggs just make the filling go further.

Pour the mixture into the pastry-lined flan dish, and bake in a fairly hot oven – 220C/425F until the filling, which will be a delicious leafy green colour, begins to acquire a golden tan. Test with a finger to make sure the filling is firm, then remove from the oven.

You can serve it hot, or cold. Or warm. Alternatively make small individual tartlets to serve as starters.

Caramelised onion tarte tatin
Finely slice 6 medium onions and put them in a cast-iron frying pan with 2 tablespoons of butter, 2 tablespoons of oil and half a teaspoon of chopped fresh thyme. Cook very, very slowly until the onions are soft and golden, then add a pinch of salt and black pepper and a dessertspoon of sugar. Continue cooking for another 3-4 minutes, then leave in the pan to cool completely.

Heat the oven to 200C/400F. When the onions are cold, cover them with a circle of pastry (puff or shortcrust, whichever you fancy), tucking it down in the pan round the edges, and bake for 30-35 minutes, until the pastry is golden brown. Lift carefully out of the oven – mind that red-hot pan and handle – and flip over onto a flat plate. Don't worry if some of the onion sticks to the pan – just scrape it off and pat it on top of the rest.

Quick pizza
No time to make a traditional pizza base? An old Fanny Cradock tip was to use a scone base instead.

For my scone mixture, I mix together 4 cups of self-raising flour, 2 teaspoons of baking powder, 1 teaspoon of salt, ¼ cup of olive oil, 2 eggs, a teaspoon of oregano and just sufficient milk to make a firm dough that you can roll out on a floured board. Makes 2 large pizzas. Top with tomato purée, sliced onions, sliced tomatoes, finely chopped red peppers, grated cheese, anchovies, peppers, capers, and bake in a hot oven 260C/500F for about 10 minutes.

No-meat Cornish pasties
These are so good and great for when you're travelling, or for picnics.

Use a pastry of your choice – I use the stirred pastry.

Process together one medium potato, 1 small onion, ½ a small swede and 2 tablespoons of stock powder until finely chopped. Add 2 tablespoons of red kidney beans. Add a good grinding of black pepper. Roll the pastry into circles about 8" in diameter, place a spoonful of filling in the centre, and crimp the edges together to form pasties. Slash a small cut in the pastry, and brush with milk. Bake for about 45 minutes at 190C/375F.
Use soya milk to brush the pastry for a vegan version

Cheese, potato and onion pie
Line a pie dish with pastry of your choice, and add 2 cups of thinly sliced boiled potatoes, 1 cup of chopped parboiled onion, and a cup of grated Cheddar cheese. Season with salt and pepper, cover with remaining pastry, and bake at 200C/400F for approximately 30 minutes, until the pastry is golden brown.

VEGETABLE DISHES

Imam bayildi
There are many versions of this lush and flavoursome dish, but they all contain the same basic ingredients – aubergine, onion, tomato, garlic and olive oil.

Cut two aubergines in half, lengthways. Score the flesh deeply with a sharp knife, and then char in a lightly-oiled very hot frying pan, pressing the flesh down hard until the aubergine begins to collapse. Remove from the pan to a large dish. Add a splash of oil to the pan and fry a sliced onion until just turning brown at the edges. Pour on two cups of tomato purée (not the paste), add half a teaspoon of salt, a generous pinch of black pepper, a teaspoon of sugar, two cloves of chopped garlic and bring to the boil. Stir in two cups of chopped coriander, a quarter of a cup of raisins or sultanas, and ¼ cup of olive oil. Pour over the aubergine and bake at 200C/400F for 30-40 minutes, until the aubergine is tender.
Vegan, gluten free

Stuffed baked tomatoes

Slice the top off some nice ripe tomatoes. Scoop out the seeds and core with a sharp or serrated teaspoon (a grapefruit spoon is perfect for this). Sprinkle with salt and pepper. Chop the core, and mix, together with the seeds, with 2 tablespoons of finely chopped spring onions, four crushed cloves of garlic, and 2 tablespoons of chopped parsley or basil. Leave to stand for half an hour, then fill the tomato shells with the mixture, and pat four tablespoons of fresh breadcrumbs over the top. Cook on the top shelf of a hot oven – 250C/475F for about 10 minutes, until the breadcrumbs are golden brown.
Vegan

Peppers and feta

Cheese and vinegar sounds like quite an odd mixture, but it works rather well and has a lovely tangy flavour.

Thinly slice some red peppers, and fry them over moderate heat in a couple of tablespoons of olive oil until they soften and turn floppy. Add a clove or two of very finely chopped garlic and stir around for a few seconds to let the garlic cook, but not brown.

Remove the pan from the heat, and sprinkle with a tablespoon of balsamic vinegar, a tablespoon of capers, and a cup of cubed Feta cheese.
Gluten free

Baked walnut balls

We're lucky enough to have a large walnut tree in the garden. Despite being blown horizontal by the great storm of 1999, it has flourished and gives a good crop of nuts every year.
For 4 people: Mix together 1 cup of finely chopped or ground walnuts, 1 cup of fresh breadcrumbs, 1 cup of grated Cheddar cheese, 1 medium onion, finely chopped, 2 tablespoons of fresh chopped parsley, 1 small jar of red peppers, well-drained and diced, and 1 beaten egg. Season with salt and pepper.

If the mixture seems too crumbly, moisten with a little milk or stock. Roll into golf ball sized rounds, and bake in a greased dish at 180C/350F for 25-30 minutes, until golden brown.

Creamed sweetcorn

We ate a lot of sweetcorn or 'mealie' in Kenya. Like artichokes, eating corn on the cob is a messy but rewarding activity. My advice is not to wear expensive clothes when you're chewing a mealie, because butter always seems to drip off and/or run down your arms, no matter how careful you are.

Sweetcorn is indelibly linked, in my mind, to Dachshunds, and this is why.

I had a very special teenage friend in Kenya, and was often invited to eat at their house where their cook made wonderful sweetcorn in a creamy cheese sauce. He cooked fresh mealies and scraped off the kernels before mixing them with the sauce.

The family had four Dachshund dogs, three males and a bitch, and the dogs ruled the house. It was bedlam, because twice a year the bitch was on heat and the three males were frantic to get to her. Also two of the males didn't get on well and would start fighting given a chance. This meant that various dogs at various times were confined to various spaces behind various doors, and getting from room to room without letting in/out the dogs that were meant to be kept in there was really very difficult indeed, because the dogs could slither through the narrowest gaps, or between one's legs, like eels, and then there would be screams, curses, snarls, growls and general pandemonium.

Whenever I think of this dish, I remember the family cook, an imperturbable man, tall and thin, wearing the typical ankle-length white kanzu and red fez that was the uniform of cooks, balancing a tray of food precariously shoulder high, while kicking his way Ninja-fashion through the dining room door with one foot and paddling with the other foot to keep the dogs out.

The recipe is very simple. You need a bowl of sweetcorn kernels, and a good helping of a rich cheese sauce, for which you can find the recipe in the Sauces and Pickles section. Mix the two together in a shallow dish and pop under a hot grill for a couple of minutes until the surface bubbles and turns golden. Serve with toast, or as a side vegetable.

Vegetarian sausages
Sausage-shaped, that's all they have in common with meat sausages. You certainly won't find any of those unpleasant lumps of gristle in them. :)

In a large bowl stir together 2 tablespoons of rolled oats, 1 cup of grated Cheddar cheese, 1 cup of wholemeal breadcrumbs, 1 large egg, a teaspoon of strong mustard, ½ teaspoon each of thyme, rosemary and sage, a grating of nutmeg and a pinch of black pepper.

Chop one large onion and fry gently in a little vegetable oil until the onion is transparent and beginning to colour round the edges. Add it to the mixture in the bowl. Mix well, and form into sausage shapes. Either bake for 15 minutes at 220C/425F, or cook under a medium grill, turning until browned on all sides.

Crustless quiche
Takes moments to make. Chop some vegetables – I use onions, red and yellow peppers, garlic and butternut squash, but you can use anything you have handy. If the vegetables are raw, cook them gently in olive oil until soft, then set them aside while you beat a couple of eggs, a handful of grated cheese and a cup of cream together (add a couple of teaspoons of mustard if you like.) Mix the vegetables in, season with salt and pepper, pour into a greased flan dish or any shallow dish, and bake at moderate temperature – 190C/375F until set and the top is beginning to turn golden, about 10 to 15 minutes.
Gluten free

Cauliflower cheese

I absolutely adore this dish, so do most people I know, apart from my son who can't abide it. It makes him gag. Just goes to show that people have different tastes.

Because cauliflower can be rather bland – they don't seem to taste the way they used to – the sauce needs to be really strong and tangy, whatever cheese you use. My preference is for an extra mature farmhouse Cheddar that bites back.

Chop the cauliflower into quarters, together with the hard stalk and any of the smaller green leaves that are in good condition. Boil or steam until a knife goes easily through the stalk.

Meanwhile put three cups of milk, ⅔ cup of flour, 1 teaspoon salt and ¼ cup butter into a saucepan, over moderate heat, and whisk gently until the sauce starts to boil and thicken. Let it cook for a few minutes, then stir in 2 heaped teaspoons of mustard and about 1 cup of grated cheese. You should have a nice thick smooth cheese sauce. Check the seasoning.

Once the cauliflower is cooked to your liking, drain it and chop it roughly in the pan. Put into an oven-proof dish and stir in the sauce. Sprinkle a couple of tablespoons of grated cheese over the top. Place under a hot grill for a few minutes, until the top is golden and bubbly.

Variation: stir in some crispy fried onions, or for meat-eaters some crispy bacon.

Ratatouille

Loads of variations on this wonderfully colourful and flavoursome Mediterranean recipe.

Start by frying some sliced onions and garlic in plenty of olive oil. When the onion is soft and transparent, add some diced aubergine (eggplant) and cook for a couple of minutes. Then

add some chopped red and green peppers, some sliced courgette (zucchini), and some skinned and chopped tomatoes. Stir over a moderate heat until the vegetables have broken down into a soft mixture, adding a little hot water if it becomes too dry. Stir in some fresh oregano or thyme, and basil, and season well. I sometimes add a few capers and black olives. Serve at room temperature.
Vegan, gluten free

Piperade

From the beautiful, wild Basque region, this is a variation on ratatouille, with the addition of egg to make it a more substantial dish.

De-seed a couple of green peppers and cut into thin strips. Skin, de-seed and chop 6-8 tomatoes, and finely chop 2 large onions. Crush a couple of cloves of garlic with the blade of a heavy knife.

Melt ¼ cup each of olive oil and butter in a heavy frying pan, and cook the onions gently until they are soft but not coloured. Add the garlic, tomatoes and peppers, herbs, salt and pepper, and leave to cook over a low heat for 20-30 minutes.

When almost all the liquid has evaporated and the vegetables are tender, beat 4 eggs thoroughly and stir into the vegetables. Keep stirring until they are well-mixed and starting to set. Turn off the heat, stir for a couple more minutes, and serve straight away.
Gluten free

Potato and mushroom ragout

Peel 6-8 medium potatoes and chop into even, bite-sized pieces. Stew two cups of chopped mushrooms in ¼ cup of butter with 4 chopped shallots and 4 chopped spring onions for 10 minutes. Add the potatoes, and sprinkle with two teaspoons of cornflour (cornstarch). Add sufficient hot stock to cover, and

simmer, uncovered, until the potatoes are tender and the liquid has evaporated to half, stirring from time to time to prevent sticking. Check seasoning. Whisk together 2 egg yolks with 2 tablespoons of wine vinegar, and stir into the pan. Serve immediately, garnished with chives.
Gluten free

Spicy butterbean bake

There are some food combinations that some people find odd. Like jam in savoury dishes. But roast pork is traditionally eaten with apple sauce, lamb with redcurrant jelly, so it isn't really that strange. The spiciness of this dish is balanced by the sweetness of the fruit. It's a non-meat version of South Africa's famous bobotie. I've tested it on South African carnivores, and it was very well received. :)

Chop two onions roughly and sauté in a little oil until they just begin to turn brown at the edges. Stir in a tablespoon of curry powder (strength according to your taste), and then add 1½ cups of cooked butterbeans (tinned work well).

Add to the mixture a grated apple, a mashed banana, a handful of sultanas or raisins, a couple of teaspoons of mango chutney or apricot jam, a splash of wine vinegar and a clove of garlic crushed into a paste with the back of a knife.

Pour into a greased oven-proof dish. Beat together ¼ cup of milk and 1 egg, and pour over the mixture. Press 4 bay leaves into the surface in a pretty pattern. Bake at 175C/350F for about half an hour, until the top is golden. Sprinkle with a few flaked almonds browned in a frying pan.
Gluten free

Italian baked aubergines

For each person, slice one aubergine lengthways into 4 slices. Pour a couple of tablespoons of olive oil into an ovenproof dish and heat to 180C/350F.

For each aubergine, mix 4 tablespoons of fresh breadcrumbs, 1 large clove of minced garlic, 2 tablespoons of Parmesan cheese, 1 tablespoon of chopped parsley and ¼ teaspoon of grated lemon zest. Mix well together.

When the oven has reached temperature, carefully remove the dish and lay the aubergine slices in it, in a single layer. Pour a little olive oil over each slice, and then distribute the breadcrumb mixture between them, pressing down firmly. Drizzle olive oil over them generously, and put into the oven on the middle shelf. After 10 minutes check to see that the crumbs are not browning too much. If so, cover with kitchen foil and continue baking for another 10-15 minutes, or until the aubergine is very soft when you stick a knife blade through it.

Couscous with sweet Moroccan sauce
Another dish cooked for us by Miguel, which was an instant hit.

First make the sauce, for which you need to slice two onions, and sauté them in half a cup of butter, together with a heaped teaspoon of cinnamon, half a teaspoon of turmeric (use saffron instead if you're feeling extravagant), a teaspoon of ground ginger, a good pinch of salt and plenty of ground black pepper. Stir it all around until the onions are soft and floppy. Add 1½ cups of water, ½ cup of sugar and 1½ cups of sultanas. Bring to the boil, then simmer for about half an hour, until the sauce is thick and creamy.

Cook your couscous according to the directions on the packet, then spread out onto a wide dish and pour the sauce into the middle. Serve immediately.

Caponata
I haven't been to Sicily yet, but I can imagine sitting up a mountain, outside an ancient shepherd's hut at a scrubbed table, looking out over the sea, with a glass of red wine, a rustic loaf,

and a dish of caponata. Until that happens, we'll continue enjoying it in the garden at home.

If you're cooking for guests, check first that they like aubergine, because we have two friends who can't eat it. They're better off with ratatouille or piperade.

This is sufficient for four people. Cut a large aubergine (eggplant) into dice-sized cubes. (Leave the skin on.) Chop a large onion, a couple of red peppers and a stick of celery into smallish pieces, and cook them gently in ¼ cup of olive oil for 5 minutes, stirring. Add the aubergine and continue cooking for another five minutes.

Add a tin of peeled plum tomatoes (or fresh if you prefer), plus two tablespoons of red wine vinegar, one tablespoon of sugar, and a crushed clove of garlic. Cook for another two minutes, and then stir in 8 black olives, chopped in half, and a tablespoon of capers. Leave to simmer very gently until the liquid has nearly evaporated, and season to taste. It can be served hot, but I think the flavours come out best at room temperature.
Vegan, gluten free

INDIAN FOOD

Curry, for me, always brings memories of life in Kenya. The quality of food there was superb beyond description. Although I sometimes enjoyed a bowl of posho (ugali) – a coarse maize meal porridge, staple diet of poor Kenyans, cooked for me by my cook as a special treat, it is the curries that I remember best.

On Sundays, as a teenager, I used to hunt regularly with the Limuru Drag Hunt – no chasing of live animals. A 'runner' was sent off dragging a sack of smelly things – offal and aniseed – over a route chosen by the Master of the Hunt. An added bonus to not hurting or killing anything was that the route was designed to take the hunt through the best of the countryside, through rivers, valleys, ridges, never a road or fence in sight.

After the hunt it was traditional for whoever was hosting it to offer lunch to all the riders. While the grooms led the horses away to roll off the sweat in sandpits, and to eat their own meals before taking the horses home, the hunt members tucked in. The meal always consisted of a selection of curries, with numerous accompaniments: rice; dahl; bowls of chopped tomato; hard-boiled egg; chutneys; lime pickle; shredded coconut; raita; chopped pineapple; peanuts; sultanas; sliced banana; poppadoms.

Once I started work, I met many Indians and was often invited to their homes to enjoy their delicious cuisine, although it took a little while to get used to the custom of the women cooking and eating their meals in the kitchen, while the men ate separately. No less than the fragrances and tastes was the warmth and friendliness of the people. The women graceful in beautiful flowing saris, the men courteous and jovial.

It was also a tradition in Nairobi to go out for a curry on Saturday evenings, usually to The Three Bells, which at the time was the most popular curry house in town. It was a mark of machismo among the males to see who could eat the hottest curry. If Vindaloo wasn't hot enough, they'd ask for Zindaloo. When I ate with Indian friends I mentioned that I wasn't very good with hot curries, and they laughed. "It's only you British who want curry so hot," they said. "It isn't meant to be blowing off your head! It's meant to be spicy flavours, not gunpowder."

The most important ingredients in the curry are the spices, and they must be really fresh, because if they're not, the curry will be flavourless and bitter and there's absolutely nothing you can do to rescue it. Believe me, I speak from 'bitter' experience.

Basic curry sauce

The basic curry sauce shown to me by my friend Urmil all those years ago is simple:

In a large saucepan, put ¼ cup of ghee (you can replace it with vegetable oil, but it doesn't give such a rich flavour). Finely chop a medium onion and fry it in the fat for a few minutes until it just begins to turn brown at the edges. Add 2 teaspoons of powdered coriander, and 1 teaspoon each of cumin, turmeric and garam masala. Stir over medium heat for 10-15 minutes so that the spices cook thoroughly, but be careful not to burn them. Then grate or finely chop a thumb sized piece of fresh ginger, crush 5 cloves of garlic and a slice a small green chilli pepper, very finely, and add them to the mixture.

Keep cooking for another 5 minutes, stirring all the time. The mixture mustn't burn, but the spices must be well cooked otherwise they will give an unpleasant raw taste to the curry. Finally add 2 cups of puréed tomatoes or ready-made passata, or 1 cup of water and 1 cup of tomato, and one teaspoon of salt. Put a lid on the saucepan and leave the sauce to cook very slowly for 45-60 minutes, checking every so often to make sure it isn't sticking. If it gets too dry, add a little water. When the sauce is ready, you should be able to see a layer of oil on the surface.

Add cooked meat, fish or vegetables to the sauce and heat through thoroughly. Alternatively, you can cook fish and vegetables in the sauce. Add plenty of chopped coriander (cilantro) to serve, and a spoonful of yoghurt.

For a creamy, mild sauce, add some cream or coconut cream to the mixture just before serving.

For a hotter, spicier curry, add more chillies and/or curry powder after frying the onion and spices.

For a richer curry, stir in a couple of tablespoons of mango chutney. If you have time, make this the day before, as the flavour improves with keeping.

The sauce is vegan if you replace the ghee with vegetable oil and omit the yoghurt, gluten free

Dhal
I love this creamy lentil dish either as an accompaniment to curry, or on its own.

Finely slice a large onion, and fry over a moderate heat in 2 tablespoons of ghee, with two cloves of chopped garlic and a teaspoon of grated ginger, until the onion begins to turn golden brown. Add ½ teaspoon of turmeric and 1 cup of red or yellow lentils or split peas. Stir over the heat for a couple of minutes, then add 3 cups of hot water. Bring to the boil, then lower the heat and simmer for 20 minutes.

Add half a teaspoon of salt and half a teaspoon of garam masala, stir thoroughly, and continue cooking over low heat until the lentils have broken down into a creamy texture and absorbed all the liquid, adding more liquid if necessary.

Meanwhile finely sliced a couple of onions and fry in ghee until they are brown and crispy, and stir into the dhal to serve.
Vegan, gluten free

Prawn Dhansak curry
Despite the rather long list of ingredients, this is very quick and easy to prepare and makes a very tasty and filling curry. This recipe makes 6 generous servings.

Rinse a cup of split red lentils and remove any little stones. Put them in a pan with three times their volume of water and a pinch of salt. Bring to the boil, then simmer until they have broken down, about 25 minutes.

Meanwhile, finely chop three large onions and fry with 3 finely chopped cloves of garlic, a heaped tablespoon of grated fresh ginger, 3 teaspoons each of coriander and cumin powder, 1½ teaspoons of garam masala and 4 teaspoons chilli powder in 3 tablespoons of ghee or vegetable oil until the onions are soft. Add two tins of chopped tomatoes, half a teaspoon of salt and 2 cups of stock. Simmer for 10-15 minutes. By now the lentils should be cooked, so drain them and add to the mixture, mixing well. Add 2-3 cups of cooked prawns, heat through thoroughly, then stir in 3 tablespoons of mango chutney and a handful of finely chopped fresh coriander.
Gluten free

Red lentil and sweet potato curry
Sauté a chopped onion in a couple of tablespoons of ghee or vegetable oil until the onion is soft and transparent. Add a peeled sweet potato cut into 1" (2.5cm) cubes, a tablespoon of grated ginger, a very finely chopped clove of garlic and a tablespoon of curry powder. Stir for a couple of minutes.

Add 3½ cups of boiling stock, a bay leaf and 1½ cups of red lentils. Cover, and simmer over a low heat for 20 minutes, by which time the lentils should be cooked and the sweet potato tender. Season to taste. Stir in 1 tablespoon of coconut oil or coconut cream, and serve sprinkled with fresh chopped coriander (cilantro).
Use oil for vegan version, gluten free

Onion bhaji
On my way to work every morning in Nairobi, between the car park and the office was a stall selling Indian street food. The aroma of fried spices was mouthwatering and irresistible, which is why I always arrived in the office with a greaseproof bag containing samosas or bhajis. Luckily my boss was similarly addicted, so the day generally started with a cup of tea and an Indian treat. What can be simpler than slicing some onions, mixing them with flour and spices, and cooking batches

in hot oil? How is that for fast food? How delicious is it served with a squeeze of lemon juice? Takes 5 minutes to prepare, 10 minutes to cook.

There are numerous recipes for onion bhaji, this is the simplest, again from my friend Urmil. Cut 3 onions in half from top to bottom, and then slice finely, and put them in a bowl. Add 1 teaspoon of chilli powder, 3 teaspoons of cumin powder, 1 teaspoon turmeric, 2 tablespoons of coriander powder and a teaspoon of salt. Stir to coat the onion with the spices. Sprinkle with chickpea flour or a mixture of rice flour and cornflour (cornstarch), just sufficient to coat the onion, and then add a little water to bind together. The onions should not be smothered in batter. Have a pan of vegetable oil ready, hot but not smoking. Drop a tiny blob of batter into the oil. If it rises to the top quickly, the temperature is right. Using two dessert spoons shape the mixture into small dumplings and slide into the fat. Cook in the oil, turning a couple of times, until golden and crispy. Drain well on kitchen paper, and serve with raita, chutney or a squeeze of lemon juice. You can vary the spices to suit your own taste.
Vegan, Gluten-free

Faux samosas
For all that I have tried, I have never been able to make a samosa I'm totally happy with. I cannot replicate the crisp, crunchy pastry that I remember, nor the way they were folded into perfect triangles, and they certainly can't be made in a limited time. But ... Thanks to lovely Leela for the many wonderful delights she shared when we worked in the same office many years ago. She always brought delicious home-made Indian treats to work and enlivened an otherwise supremely boring job. I sometimes think some of us only stayed there because of Leela and her food. One of the best things were her 'cheat's samosas' which everybody loved. They are incredibly simple to make. You just need some left-

over curry, some chutney or jam, a sliced loaf, and a sandwich toaster.

Spread some of the curry onto a slice of bread. Add a dollop of mango chutney or any fruity jam. Place another slice of bread on top to make a sandwich. Brush both slices of bread with a little oil or melted butter, and cook in the sandwich toaster. In no time at all you have perfect little packages, which taste equally good cold or hot.
Vegan - coat bread with oil, not butter

Spicy eggplant in yoghurt
This is a gorgeous accompaniment to curry, both spicy and creamy, as a buffet dish, or as a snack with some naan bread.

Heat sufficient oil in a large pan so that it is 2-3 inches deep. While the oil is heating, cut a large unpeeled aubergine (eggplant) into cubes about 3/4" (2.0 cm). Put the pieces into a plastic bag and add a teaspoon of salt, a teaspoon of turmeric, and a pinch of chilli powder. (The amount of chilli powder you use depends on how hot you like your dishes.) Shake the bag until the cubes are evenly coated in the mixture.

When the oil is sizzling hot, add the cubes a handful at a time and fry for a couple of minutes until they are golden brown. Remove with a slotted spoon and drain on kitchen paper.

While they are cooling, finely slice an onion, crush two cloves of garlic, finely chop a small green chilli, grate a teaspoon of fresh ginger, and mix with a cup of plain yoghurt, half a teaspoon of English mustard, a generous pinch of sugar and a tablespoon of vinegar.

Mix in the aubergine and leave at room temperature until ready to serve.
Gluten free

Tandoori salmon
Cut salmon into bite-size pieces. Mix together 4 tablespoons of yoghurt, a tablespoon of lemon juice, a 1" (2.5cm) piece of fresh ginger, grated, 2 cloves of crushed garlic, 1 teaspoon each of cumin, coriander, garam masala, chilli powder and tandoori curry powder and ½ a teaspoon of salt. Marinade the salmon in the sauce for at least an hour, and then cook in a very hot oven – 280C/530F for 10 minutes.
Serve with plain boiled rice
Gluten free

Prawns in green masala sauce
Blend 1 small onion, 1 clove of garlic, a handful of fresh coriander leaves, a handful of mint leaves (or a soup spoon of mint sauce), half a green pepper and 1-2 chillies with half a cup coconut milk. Cook fresh prawns in hot melted ghee in a large frying pan for 2-3 minutes, then add the puréed mixture and simmer for 10-15 minutes. Or use cooked prawns, and add to the purée mixture 5 minutes before the end of cooking time.
Gluten free

Prawns Masala
Sauté a thumb-sized piece of chopped ginger, 2 cloves of crushed garlic and a large pinch of turmeric in a couple of tablespoons of ghee or vegetable oil for a couple of minutes. Add 4 large chopped onions and cook gently until they turn golden brown. Add 4 cups of peeled prawns with ½-1 teaspoon of chilli powder, stir well and add a cup of water and a pinch of salt. Lower the heat and simmer until prawns are cooked, about 3-4 minutes. When water has nearly evaporated add 1 teaspoon of garam masala, a grinding of black pepper and 1 cup of chopped coriander. Serve with cucumber raita, rice and chapatis.
Gluten free

Lemon rice
Wash a lemon thoroughly, cut into quarters and remove the pips. Blend with 3 cups of water into a smooth pulp, and then

strain off the liquid, discarding the pulp. If necessary add more water to make up 3 full cups. Bring the liquid to the boil, add a good pinch of salt and cook 1 cup of long grain rice with the lid on, until tender.
Vegan, gluten free

Fragrant coconut rice
In a large saucepan bring to the boil 4½ cups of coconut milk, ½ teaspoon of black pepper, 1 teaspoon of grated lemon zest, ½ teaspoon of grated nutmeg, ½ teaspoon of ground cloves, a couple of curry leaves and 1½ teaspoons of salt. Stir in 2 cups of basmati rice, turn the heat right down, cover and leave to cook for 15-20 minutes.
Vegan, gluten free

9

Fish Dishes

Mrs Nextdoor, my kind, generous, funny neighbour, is pulling lettuce from her vegetable garden, while I am hanging out the washing. It is late morning, shortly before noon. She hands me a lettuce and some courgettes, and asks if I'd like some rabbit – they raise their own meat.

I thank her and say I don't eat meat.

She looks puzzled.

"When? On Fridays, for religious reasons?"

"No, never."

Her expression changes to horror. She actually raises a hand to her mouth in shock.

"But cherie, if you don't eat meat you'll be very ill."

I laugh.

"I haven't eaten it for 30 years."

Her voice rises to a squeal.

"30 years! Mon dieu, how is that? And yet you look so healthy."

She shakes her head as if she cannot equate not eating meat with looking healthy.

When we have been invited out by new friends, especially French friends, I've caught the flicker of panic in their eyes as they silently struggle with the idea of a meatless meal. "But what do you eat?" they ask. "Are you a vegan? What is the difference between vegans and vegetarians?"

France is only slowly getting up to speed where vegetarians and vegans are concerned. Ask if there is anything on the menu that doesn't contain meat, and you may be offered a nice slice of quiche – only to find *'lardons'* – diced bacon in it. Bacon, like sausage, salami, chorizo and poultry is not meat, they will explain. Meat is only slabs of steak, or a pork chop. :) But if you don't like it, just eat the rest and leave those bits, they suggest.

Is the vegetable soup vegetarian? *Mais oui*, Madame. What is the stock made from? Chicken bones, Madame. Um, it isn't vegetarian if the stock has been made from bones. Nothing is vegetarian if it contains any trace of meat.

Although vegetarians eat dairy products like butter, cheese and yoghurt, these are a by-product of the meat industry, because cattle, sheep and goats generally only produce milk when they have given birth to young. (There are exceptions, known as maiden milkers, they are fairly rare.) Therefore the majority of male calves, lambs and kids will go to slaughter, having served their purpose which is to make their mothers produce milk for human consumption. Cheese is formed by the addition of rennet to the milk – rennet being a substance taken from the stomach of calves. There are vegetarian alternatives, but they are more difficult to find. Liberal vegetarians will eat meat when it would be too rude not and they want to avoid offending people. Others would have to refuse because the

87

thought is anathema to them. (It is to me too, but there are occasions when we have to overcome certain feelings out of respect for others.) Strict vegetarians only eat vegetarian cheese, and avoid things like Worcestershire sauce, which contains anchovies.

Vegans reject any form of food that results from the death or exploitation of any living creature. As well as not eating meat, they do not eat dairy products, eggs or honey; nor do they wear silk, derived from silkworms, nor wool.

Hens naturally lay eggs. Unless they are fertilised they will never develop into chicks. Taking them away does not cause distress to the hen, nor does cooking the unfertilised egg kill a living being. I am happy to eat eggs as long as they come from hens who live a natural life, in natural surroundings. The yolk of an egg from a free-range chicken is rich and golden, unlike those of hens kept in cages, stacked upon each other so that the lower ones are pasted with the faeces of those above them, kept in artificial lighting to make them lay twice daily, and whose miserable life span is mercifully short.

Although we don't eat meat, we do regularly eat fish. There's a belief that fish is better undercooked than overcooked. Well, for me, it's the opposite. If it's still transparent inside, I can't swallow it. I'd rather it was burnt! Ideally, it's cooked thoroughly but still moist. I test it by poking a sharp knife into the thickest part. If there's a hint of transparency, it's not sufficiently well done for my taste. And I prefer fish dishes that don't taste too fishy. I'm just not keen on overtly smelly fish or too strong a fishy flavour, so I generally enfold or smother it in a highly-flavoured sauce. And no matter how I've cooked them, I've never managed to make those frozen grey bricks called 'fillets' edible.

Of all the fish we eat, salmon is top of my list. These are all favourite recipes, and none of them in-your-face fishy. I always ask the fishmonger to clean the fish for me, as it's something I really don't enjoy, and generally choose fillets over whole fish, as they're easier to serve and eat. Several of our friends won't eat anything with bones or skin.

Fish in coconut and apple sauce

To make the sauce, finely chop a large onion, and cook in a couple of tablespoons of oil until soft and colouring round the edges. Peel and core two cooking apples, cut into chunks and add to the pan with ¾ of a cup of coconut cream, ½ teaspoon of salt, 1 teaspoon of sugar, 2 teaspoons of curry powder, 2 teaspoons of coriander powder, 1 teaspoon of cumin powder and ½ pint of stock. Bring to the boil, cover and simmer very gently for 15 minutes, stirring from time to time.

Blend to a smooth purée, and then add fillets of firm white fish, cut into chunks, and simmer for 10 minutes until the fish flakes. Garnish with chopped parsley, and serve with boiled rice.

Gluten free

Milanese-style fish

My first mother-in-law came from northern Italy, and this is one of the ways she used to cook fish fillets. She used tilapia, a particularly tasty fish which was easily obtainable in Kenya where we lived, but you can use any firm fleshed fillets. Check carefully for bones.

Allow 1 fillet per person. Finely chop a small onion, and mix with the juice of one lemon, 2 tablespoons olive oil, a good pinch of salt and a sprinkle of black pepper. Put the fillets in a dish and pour the mixture over, leaving the fish to stand for 1-2 hours.

When ready to cook, dip the fillets into flour, then into beaten egg, and finally into fresh breadcrumbs. Fry in a large heavy frying pan over gentle heat, in a mixture of butter and olive oil. After 3-4 minutes turn carefully and fry on the other side.

Serve either with a few capers, a squeeze of lemon juice, or with caper and parsley dressing (Recipe in the Sauces and Pickles section.)

Sizzled salmon in mango sauce

For a quick and tasty dish, whizz up a can of mango slices (or a couple of fresh mangoes) with a cup of white wine. Fry your salmon cutlets or fillets - if you are keeping the skin on, fry skin side down first - in very hot oil until the salmon is visibly crispy and brown, and if you stick a knife through it, it is cooked through. Quickly heat the mango/wine mixture in a saucepan. Pour the purée onto a plate, and lay the salmon on top. The tangy fruit makes a good contrast with the rich fish. Good with sauté potatoes.

Gluten free

Venetian sole

There is no fishy smell to this unusual dish which is served on special occasions in Venice. It's useful in that it can be prepared in advance.

You need one to two fillets of sole per person, depending on whether you are serving as a starter or main course.

Put the fillets in a plastic bag with a couple of tablespoons of flour and a teaspoon of salt, and turn gently to coat the fish. Shake off any surplus flour, then fry the fillets over a moderate heat in a mixture of hot olive oil and butter, or all butter, adding a handful of sultanas and a handful of pine nuts.

When the fillets are golden brown remove the fish, sultanas and pine nuts to a dish, and fry a couple of thinly sliced onions in the fat until they are a dark golden brown. Add the onions to the fish. Pour over about one-third of a cup of red wine vinegar, and leave the fish to stand for a couple of hours before serving.

Scallops with Pernod and cream

Pat scallops dry with kitchen towel, and then turn them over in a plastic bag with two tablespoons of flour and a good pinch of salt and pepper. Shake off any excess flour, then cook the scallops in butter over high heat until golden brown - should only take a couple of minutes.

Pour over half a wine glass of Pernod and set light to it, either by tilting it into the flame of the gas, or by using a match. Swirl it around until the flame goes out, then add a cup of double cream. Simmer for a few minutes until the cream becomes thick and shiny. Garnish with freshly chopped chives and serve with plain boiled rice.
Variation: Cook some very finely sliced fennel in butter until tender, and add to the pan with the cream.

Simple fish pie
This is the way my cook in Kenya made fish pie.

Lay 4-6 fish fillets in a well-greased oven-proof dish. Cover with a layer of sliced tomatoes, a layer of bechamel sauce, a layer of finely sliced onions, and top with a layer of creamy mashed potatoes.

Bake for about 1 hour at 180C/350F, until the potato topping is golden brown.

Sticky salmon steaks
This fishy alternative to sticky ribs was a popular supper dish at Sandy's, made by a silent gentleman with a long beard who never spoke, whether because he couldn't or didn't wish to, but he was a great cook. He appeared from time to time and helped Sandy with her patients. We didn't know his name, so we called him Jeremy and he didn't seem to mind.

He also showed me how to chop and slice onions, by cutting them in half lengthways then peeling back the skin to the root and using it as a handle to hold the onion still.

In a fairly large pan (because the mixture will bubble up) put 1⅓ cups (one can) Coca Cola, ½ cup tomato ketchup, ½ cup

sugar, ¼ cup Worcestershire sauce and 1 tablespoon of balsamic vinegar. Bring to the boil and allow to simmer until reduced by about half, and thickened. Stir from time to time. The result is a beautiful deep mahogany colour sticky sauce, sufficient for about 4 steaks. Put salmon steaks into an ovenproof dish, pour over the sauce, turn them once to make sure all sides are covered, and bake in a hot oven – 250C/475F — for 15 minutes. You can equally use this sauce for spare ribs or chicken wings.
Gluten free

Lush lemon salmon
A way to give salmon steaks real tangy zing.

Put 4 tablespoons of stock, 4 tablespoons of lemon juice, the grated rind of half a lemon and 2 tablespoons of sugar in a pan over medium heat until the sugar dissolves, then bring up to the boil. Stir in 1 tablespoon of water mixed with ½ tablespoon of cornflour (cornstarch) until the sauce is thick and glossy. Season to taste.

Serve with poached or grilled salmon steaks.
Gluten free

Fish fillets in cheese crust
This is another mother-in-law dish, and the way I often cook white fish fillets.

Mix equal quantities of fresh breadcrumbs and grated Parmesan cheese with a crushed clove of garlic and some salt and pepper. Dry fillets with kitchen paper, then dip first in beaten egg and then in the breadcrumb mixture. Fry on each side until fish is cooked through, depending on the thickness of the fillet, in a pan of sizzling butter and olive oil over moderate heat. Pour any remaining fat over the fillets to serve. She used the same recipe for chicken breasts, which she skinned and flattened with a rolling pin.

Rich fish pie
I love this dish in the depths of winter, eating it from our laps in front of the television. There's something comforting and almost luxurious about it. This makes enough for two.

Peel two large potatoes and cut into chunks. Boil in salted water until tender, then drain and mash with a good knob of butter.

Put 4 white fish fillets, half a sliced onion, a sliced carrot and a cup of frozen peas into a pan with 2 cups of milk. Bring up to the boil, then cover the pan and remove from the heat and take the fish and vegetables out of the milk with a slotted spoon. Put them in an oven-proof dish (add a handful of cooked prawns to make the pie even tastier.)

Melt a tablespoon of butter in a pan, and add a tablespoon of flour. Stir over gentle heat for a few minutes until the mixture becomes grainy, then whisk in the milk that the fish and vegetables were cooked in. Bring to the boil and cook for a couple of minutes until the sauce thickens. Season well with salt and pepper. Pour over the fish and vegetables.

Cover with the mashed potato, sprinkle with a little grated Cheddar cheese, and bake at 200C/400F for 20-30 minutes, until the potato is golden.

Smoked salmon quiche
Thanks to Janet for this very rich and delicious quiche.

To serve 6, line a 9" quiche dish with pastry made with 1½ cups of flour.
Sauté a large onion in 1 tablespoon of oil until soft and golden, and set aside to cool.

Whisk together 2 eggs, ¾ of a cup of cream cheese and 2 tablespoons of soft goats' cheese until smooth. Whisk in 1 cup of single cream, and add 1 tablespoon of chopped thyme or dill. Season with salt and pepper. Scatter the cooked onions and 1 cup of smoked salmon trimmings over the pastry, pour the egg mixture on top, and bake at 175C/350F for 45-55 minutes. Serve warm or cold.

Smoked salmon roulade

Very impressive to look at, and not that difficult to make. It's like a savoury Swiss roll. Worth the slight effort required. Recipe courtesy of my friend Sonia, one of the best cooks I know.

You need a Swiss roll tin, which you grease and then line with greased greaseproof paper. Don't take any chances with the roll sticking!

Heat the oven to 200C/400F.

Melt ¼ cup of butter over gentle heat, then stir in ½ cup plain flour. Stir together for a few minutes until the butter has absorbed all the flour. Remove from the heat and gradually stir in 1 cup of milk. Put it back over the heat and bring to the boil, whisking until the mixture thickens. Stir in the yolks of 4 eggs, ¾ cup of grated Cheddar cheese, and 2 teaspoons of chopped dill.

Now beat 4 egg whites until they hold their shape and form gentle peaks, and carefully fold into the cheese mixture. Spread it over the greaseproof paper evenly, and bake until set and golden, about 10-12 minutes.

Remove from the oven and turn the roll out gently onto a clean tea towel on a wire rack. Carefully peel off the greaseproof paper. That's the fussy bit done.

While the roll is cooking mix together 1 cup of cream cheese with chives and onions, 1 cup of chopped smoked salmon and

1 teaspoon of finely grated lemon zest. Spread it over the cooled roll. Roll up the roll and glow with pride. It's equally good hot or cold, and will serve 6 people generously.

Trout
Trout has such a beautiful, delicate flavour, I think it is best served as simply as possible.

Allow one fillet per person. Put a couple of tablespoons of flour and half a teaspoon of salt and pepper in a clear plastic bag. Shake it around for a moment to distribute the seasoning. Put the fillets into the bag and turn them around gently to coat them in the mixture.

Heat a tablespoon of butter and a tablespoon of oil over medium-high heat until it begins to foam. Lay the floured fillets in the fat and let them cook for 2-3 minutes on each side until golden brown. Remove the fish from the pan, add the juice of half a lemon to the fat and swirl around for a few seconds, then pour over the fish and sprinkle with chopped parsley. It also works well if you add a dessertspoon of capers to the butter, and instead of lemon juice a little cream stirred into the fat.

10

Potato Dishes

Imagine a world without potatoes. How sad would that be?
They are undoubtedly the most versatile vegetable ever grown,
and we love them. No excuse here for the number of recipes,
and that's why they have a whole chapter to themselves.

I hope you don't throw away your potato peelings? Because
as long as you wash the potatoes very thoroughly before
peeling, they make wonderful crisps. Just dry them well on
kitchen towel and fry in hot oil for a few minutes until they
start to turn pale golden colour. Bingo!

New potatoes
Is there anybody who doesn't love a plate of baby new
potatoes? Washed well and boiled in their skins, oh, how lovely

they are. We love them with melted butter and chopped parsley or mint, or melted butter and a few capers.
Gluten free

I hate micro-baked potatoes!
There – I've said it. In my opinion it takes great skill, or a microwave oven, to ruin a potato. A baked potato has to have a golden, crispy, crunchy skin – that's the best part – that you can cut a cross in and squeeze to create a fluffy interior and fill with butter or grated cheese or baked beans or whatever you fancy. Every microwaved potato I've ever eaten has had a thin papery skin and rather unpleasant fibrous interior.

I use my tabletop halogen oven for baking potatoes, as it is economical on electricity and does a very good job. I place the washed potatoes on a sheet of foil and dribble olive oil over them, then sprinkle with salt, and cook at a high temperature until the skins are well browned and a sharp knife meets no resistance when stabbed into the potato.

I watched in dismay as a friend, invited for supper, carefully scooped out all the fluffy part of the potatoes and left the golden crispy wonderfulness of the skins on the side of the plate. I had to sit on my hands not to reach out and grab them!
Gluten free

Aligote and Truffade
Both peasant dishes from the volcanic heart of France, the Auvergne region.

Think of Aligote as mashed potatoes with melted cheese – preferably a young Tome stirred into the very hot mashed potatoes make a deliciously goo.

Truffade is thinly sliced or cubed potatoes, cooked until tender and golden, with little pieces of cheese sprinkled on them to melt. Although it is sometimes bedecked with lardons, it's one

of those rare French meals that often doesn't contain any meat but is still recognised proudly as a speciality. I love it either way. Of course, I love potatoes and cheese any way at all!
Gluten free

Sautéed potatoes
This method is best made using old, floury potatoes. Boil them for about 15 minutes in salted water, until they are still very firm. Then drain them thoroughly and dry on kitchen paper.

Cut them into slices about 1/4" (0.50cm) thick, and fry in a mixture of oil and butter over a moderate heat until golden and crispy, stirring them from time to time to stop from catching and ensure they are evenly cooked. You need a large pan, or cook them in batches, as they need to all be in contact with the fat. When they are golden and crispy on the outside, sprinkle with finely chopped garlic. Cook for a further minute, then remove from heat. Don't have the fat too hot, otherwise the outsides will burn before the insides are soft.

Drain on kitchen paper, and sprinkle with salt, pepper and chopped parsley or chives.
Gluten free

Braised potatoes
Peel and dice 10 -12 potatoes.

Melt 2 tablespoons of butter in an oven proof dish. Mix potatoes with ¾ of a pint hot stock, salt, pepper and bay leaf.

Cover, and place in oven at 180C/350F for 1½ - 2 hours, until all the liquid is absorbed.
Gluten free

Stewed potatoes with lemon and garlic
Our Greek hostess (the one who gave me the hummus recipe) also shared her recipe for lemon and garlic stewed potatoes.

For four people, you need about 8 large potatoes, peeled and cut into bite sized chunks. Put them in a large saucepan with 2 cups of hot stock, ½ a cup of olive oil, or butter, or a mixture of both, the juice of one lemon, 2 cloves of finely chopped garlic, a bay leaf, a teaspoon of salt, and a good grinding of black pepper.

Cover the pan and cook very slowly, until the potatoes are tender and most of the liquid has evaporated. Check from time to time to make sure the potatoes aren't sticking. Sprinkle with parsley to serve.
Gluten free

Potato gratin
For 4 people allow 8-12 potatoes. The final texture will depend on whether you use floury or waxy potatoes, both work well and give different results. Peel and slice very, very thin – as close to transparent as you can get. Take two cloves of garlic and whack them with a heavy knife blade to squash them and remove the skin, then rub over a shallow oven-proof dish. Put the potatoes and garlic in a large saucepan, sprinkle with plenty of salt and pepper and a good grinding of nutmeg. Cover with double cream, and bring to the boil. Simmer for two minutes, stirring with a wooden spoon to prevent sticking. Now fish around until you find the garlic, and remove it. Tip the mixture into the prepared dish, shaking it so that the potatoes settle into a thin layer, no more than 1" in depth and are covered with the cream.

Bake in a hot oven – 250C/475F – until the top is deep golden brown, about 40 minutes. The potatoes should be very soft when prodded with a knife. If the top begins to brown too quickly, cover with aluminium foil. If the dish looks too dry, add a little milk. Once the dish is cooked, leave it to cool down for 10-15 minutes before serving.

Variations:
Add grated Gruyere or Emmental cheese layered between the potatoes and/or sprinkled on top.

Replace the nutmeg and cheese with finely sliced onion between the layers.

Add a teaspoon of crushed juniper berries to the cream.
Gluten free

Boulangere potatoes
Thinly slice a couple of onions and sweat in a mixture of 2 tablespoons of butter and two tablespoons of oil, until the onions are a light golden colour. Peel and very thinly slice half a dozen potatoes. Grease an ovenproof dish and place alternate layers of potato and onion, seasoning each layer well with salt, pepper and fresh thyme leaves, adding the fat the onions were cooked in. Pour in sufficient hot stock to cover the vegetables, and bake at 200C/400F for 30-40 minutes, until the potatoes are tender and all the liquid has been absorbed.
Use all oil for a vegan version, gluten free

Cheese and potato pie
One of our friends has travelled all over the world and eaten at the best and most exclusive restaurants, but his taste in food remains as basic as it gets. Egg and chips; baked potato and beans, shepherd's pie. I used to find feeding him really, really stressful as he is completely resistant to trying anything new, and there are so many things he won't eat, or even taste. Happily I found the solution, as there is one dish he will eat seven days a week. Cheese and potato pie, made like this – no straying from the basic recipe!

Make a heap of creamy mashed potato. Season well with salt and pepper. Stir in a couple of handfuls of chopped spring onions, plenty of grated Cheddar cheese, and pack into an ovenproof dish. Cover with a layer of sliced tomatoes, and sprinkle a generous amount of grated Cheddar over the top.

Bake in a hot oven – 250C/475F, until the topping is golden and bubbling.
Gluten free

Potato gnocchi

There's no point in pretending that this isn't a bit of a messy dish to prepare, but it is delicious and children love helping! It's one of my daughter's favourite recipes, too.

Use a dozen floury potatoes to serve 4. (Don't use waxy or new potatoes – it won't work).

Peel and boil the potatoes until tender, then drain well and either mash or put through a sieve for a very smooth finish. It's very important that you work quickly so that the potatoes are still very hot when you add the remaining ingredients, as it helps to cook the flour. My mother-in-law always cooked the potatoes in their skins and then peeled them straight from the boiling water, but I don't have her asbestos fingers and by the time I can hold the potatoes, they've cooled down.

Add ½ a cup of flour, ½ a cup of grated Parmesan cheese, 3 eggs, salt, pepper and grated nutmeg. Mix together to form a dough. You may have to add more flour if the dough is very sticky. Leave the mixture to cool.

On a well-floured board, take handfuls of the mixture and roll it into a 'snake' about 1/2" (1.0 cm) in diameter. Cut the snake into 1" (2.5cm) lengths, press the back of a fork into each one, and drop into a large saucepan of simmering salted water. As the gnocchi rise to the surface, remove and keep warm in a low oven until they are all cooked. Serve with melted butter and more grated Parmesan, or a tomato sauce.

101

11

A Few Words About Vegetables

There's a very chic French businesswoman I meet from time to time. She looks as if she has just stepped out of the pages of Vogue, immaculate from the crest of her golden hair down to her perfectly-varnished toenails. We were talking about the cost of food, and I mentioned that the local supermarket were charging almost 2 Euros (around US$2) for a cauliflower, where in England they could be bought from farm shops for less than £1(around US$1.50). She looked at me in amazement. But surely I didn't buy fresh vegetables, she asked. How did I know they were REALLY fresh? Perhaps they had been picked many days before and kept in a cold place to make them look fresh. What about all the stalks and leaves you paid for and had to throw away or feed to the animals? And, horror of horrors, what about *les petites bestioles* – the little bugs! She shuddered dramatically and elegantly. Wherever possible she bought frozen vegetables, harvested and frozen the same day, hence fresh. As she pointed out, not only are they fresh, you can use however much you want and put the rest back in the freezer. I've followed her advice ever since with things like green beans, spinach, mushrooms, carrots, broccoli, cauliflower that freeze so well.

I can't think of one vegetable I don't like. Well, maybe raw celery. That's more to do with its texture than its taste, I think. I once swallowed one of the stringy outside bits, it went down my throat and lodged there, and I had to pull it out like a small snake, gagging noisily. This happened to be at a company dinner in a 5-star hotel.

We like our vegetables plain, with just a little butter, some chopped herbs, maybe a sprinkle of lemon juice or, for special treats, with my favourite luxury ingredient, truffle oil. I think vegetables are such things of beauty that they are best served in their natural state. When cooking plain vegetables such as beans, cabbage, broccoli, carrots as an accompaniment, I generally simply steam them in a colander over a pan of boiling water until they are just tender, then dress with a knob of butter or a sauce. A steamer is one of the few kitchen gadgets I've managed to resist, because I find the pan and colander method so quick and easy to use and wash, with nothing extra to store.

12

Sauces and Pickles

I love the sight of jars of home-made pickles sitting on the shelf. It makes me feel like a domestic goddess. They are so useful for adding to salads and cheese courses, and sometimes I just like a spoonful on a piece of toast. They make nice and welcome little gifts for friends and hostesses, and unopened last for years, improving with age. Like me.

Quick and easy bechamel sauce
The classic way to make a bechamel sauce involves melting the butter, stirring in the flour, adding the milk slowly while stirring all the time to prevent lumps, which it never seemed to do for me. I make mine the quicker, easier way, as taught to me by Abby.

3 cups of cold milk
⅓ of a cup of flour
¼ of a cup of cold butter

Put all the ingredients into a cold saucepan and bring slowly to the boil, whisking methodically to stop lumps forming. You can read a book or magazine while you're doing this, if you like. When the sauce begins to thicken, stir briskly for a few moments. Season with salt and pepper. Bingo!

Rich cheese sauce
Follow the recipe for bechamel sauce, adding 1 heaped teaspoon of hot mustard and a handful of grated cheese once the sauce begins to thicken.

Mayonnaise
You can go the long way round and make it by adding the oil drip by drip and risking it splitting, or take the quick route and make it in a food processor. Guess which I do?

I've always used the recipe from the brilliant Michael Barry's Complete Crafty Cookbook. As 'Michael Barry' he was a regular presenter of the BBC Good Food programme. He also presented a classical music programme on television under his real name, Michael Bukht, something that confused me enormously as I didn't realise it was the same person. How odd, I thought, these two men look and sound identical.

To make the mayonnaise, put a whole egg, a large pinch of salt, ½ a teaspoon of sugar, ½ a teaspoon of French mustard and 2 teaspoons of lemon juice in the food processor, and whizz for 10 seconds. Measure out 1 cup of salad oil and add one-quarter of it to the processor, whizzing it for another 5 seconds. Then pour in the rest, slowly, in a thin stream, with the motor running. As the mayonnaise thickens, you'll hear a change in the tone of the mixer and the mixture will become shiny.

*NEVER use extra virgin olive oil if you are using the processor method. It will produce an inedible result, horribly bitter and metallic. That's because the blades chop up the olive oil drops and they release an unpleasant and very bitter taste.

Instead use an oil like sunflower or corn oil for at least half the oil quantity, and add the olive oil once the mayonnaise has started to emulsify. Unless, of course, you like a very bitter mayonnaise. Some people do.*

*Gluten free *Raw egg**

Oriental plum sauce
You need a liquidiser to make this tangy sauce which goes well with vegetarian sausages and with grilled oily fish like salmon and mackerel. Process together ½ cup plum jam, ½ teaspoon stock powder, ½ teaspoon mustard, ¼ teaspoon of allspice and 2 tablespoons of wine vinegar.

Vegan, gluten free

Caper and parsley dressing
Another of Mamma's recipes, which goes well with hot or cold fish or meat.

Whisk, or shake together, 5 tablespoons of olive oil with 2 tablespoons of lemon juice. Stir in 1 tablespoon of chopped parsley and 2 tablespoons of drained capers.

Vegan, gluten free

Pili pili hoho
This was a standard condiment on Kenyan settlers' dining tables, and each cook would have his own particular way of preparing it, some more elaborate than others. But at its simplest, it was a small glass bottle containing either dry sherry or vinegar, with a sliced red-hot chilli pepper in it. You gave the bottle a good shake, then sprinkled just a few drops in the soup, stew or on scrambled eggs to give the dish a real kick.

Vegan, gluten free

Vegan mayonnaise
I've experimented with several recipes for an egg-free mayonnaise, and found this gives the best result and most 'lifelike' mayonnaise.

Grind a couple of tablespoons of flax seeds (linseeds) into a powder. Add 6 tablespoons of cold water, and bring to the boil, stirring continually until the mixture thickens and becomes a glutinous blob. Did you ever see that film with Steve McQueen about a blob of stuff that fell out of the sky and swallowed people? If so, that's what it looks like. But don't worry, this is safe. Set it aside to cool to room temperature.

Put the cooled mixture in a food processor (or you can use a deep jar and hand blender), and add one tablespoon of vegetable oil. (I use mainly sunflower, with a little olive oil). Just one tablespoon. Blend for 15 seconds. Now add another tablespoon of oil, and repeat the process. Keep on adding one tablespoon of oil at a time and processing for 10-15 seconds before adding the next spoonful until you have incorporated approximately 1 cup of oil. By now you will have – provided you added the oil slowly – a thick glossy emulsion which is the basis for your mayonnaise.

Flavour it to your taste with vinegar or lemon juice; mustard; sugar; capers; garlic, herbs and spices, tasting as you go until you have your perfect, thick, creamy egg-free mayonnaise.
Vegan, gluten free

Lemon & fig chutney
This is a ferocious chutney, sharp and spicy with bitter undertones. It goes well with a strong cheese and kills all known germs. Dead.

Chop or process 4-5 lemons and 1-2 cups of dried figs (you can substitute sultanas, raisins, prunes) into small pieces. Put in large saucepan with 3 cups of sugar, 1½ cups vinegar, 12 cloves, 12 peppercorns. 2 teaspoons of salt and 6 small red chillies. (If you're organised and have a piece of muslin to tie the spices in a little bag, it's easier to remove them before bottling. Otherwise you'll have to do what I do and fish around to find them.)

Bring to the boil and cook gently until the mixture begins to thicken and the lemon rind is soft. It takes between 50-60 minutes. You'll know if it's done if you drop a smidgin on a cold plate and when you push it with your finger after 10 seconds it should be sticky, not runny. If it takes too long to thicken, you can add 4 gr of agar agar to a wineglass of cold water, pour into the mixture and let it boil for 2 minutes. That will thicken it as it cools down.

Pour into warm sterilised jars. Makes 4-5 jars.

Vegan, gluten free

Peanut butter

Peanuts, whole peanuts and nothing but peanuts. With a food processor it's easy to make your own peanut butter, free of any unwelcome additions like palm oil. Fill the bowl of the processor half way, with the blade, and pulse for 5 minutes or so to break up the nuts. Then let the processor run and chop the nuts. If your processor is a bit of a wimp, like mine, give it a rest every few minutes to stop it going up in smoke. Gradually the oil will start to appear from the nuts, and it will become easier to blend. Make the butter as chunky or smooth as you please, depending on how long you blend it. Pour into clean jars. It keeps forever, if given a chance.

Vegan, gluten free

Plum chutney

Wash, halve and stone 8 cups of plums. Place in a large pan with 8 cups of skinned, sliced tomatoes and 1½ pints of vinegar and simmer slowly until the fruit is soft. Add 2 cups of chopped peeled onions, 10 cups of peeled and cored apples, 4 cloves of garlic and 2 cups of any dried fruit. Add 1½ tablespoons of mixed pickling spice in a muslin bag, 4 cups of demerara sugar and 4 level teaspoons of salt. Simmer very gently until very tender and thickened – about 2 hours, stirring from time to prevent sticking. Remove the spice and pour into sterilised jars.

Vegan, gluten free

Apricot chutney
Soak 3 cups of dried apricots in water overnight. Drain, and put in a pan with 2 large chopped onions, 1 tablespoon of coarse salt, ½ a pint of white vinegar, ¾ of a cup of demerara sugar, ½ a cup of sultanas and 1 teaspoon of allspice. Cook over gentle heat, stirring from time to time until the mixture has thickened to the consistency of jam. Test with a drop on a cold plate. The apricots should retain their shape. Store in sterilised jars.
Vegan, gluten free

Lemon butter sauce
Delicious, fast and simple, perfect with fish and vegetables.

Put the juice of half a lemon, a knob of butter and a pinch of salt in a small pan, and heat rapidly until the butter melts, swirling the pan all the time. The mixture will quickly start to bubble up as the lemon juice evaporates. That's when you know it's ready. Pour over your fish and/or vegetables, and sprinkle with freshly-ground black pepper.
Gluten free

Sweet chilli jam
Put 4 sweet red peppers, two small hot red chilli peppers and 3 cloves of garlic in the food processor and chop into a mush.

Put into a saucepan with ½ a cup of lemon juice and ½ a cup of white vinegar. Bring to the boil, and then add 4 cups of white sugar. Dissolve 1 teaspoon of agar agar (vegetarian gelatine substitute) in half a cup of water, then add to the mixture. Boil for 2 minutes and then test to see if it is ready to set, by dropping a small amount onto a cold saucer. Leave for 1 minute and the push with a finger, when the mixture should be sticky, not runny. The mixture should thicken as it cools; if it doesn't, add another teaspoon of agar agar and bring to the boil again for two minutes.
Vegan, gluten free

Courgette (zucchini) pickle

Every summer we have a real glut of courgettes (zucchini) – even if we don't plant any. They often seed themselves, and one plant produces more fruit than we know what to do with. Friends and neighbours are faced with similar situations and are always trying to off-load their surplus. :) This is one way I deal with it thanks to a recipe from Paul, and the resulting pickle goes wonderfully with cheese.

Wash 4 courgettes and cut them into very thin slices, and add one onion very finely sliced. Put in a bowl with a heaped tablespoon of salt, and cover with water. Leave aside for an hour or two, then drain, rinse and dry on a clean tea towel.

Bring to the boil two cups of apple cider vinegar, ½ a cup of brown sugar, 2 teaspoons of mustard powder, 2 teaspoons of mustard seeds and a teaspoon of turmeric powder. Simmer gently for 5 minutes, then leave to cool to room temperature. Pour the liquid over the courgettes, and put into sterilised jars. Keep for a couple of days before opening.
Vegan, gluten free

Mustard melon pickle

Remove the rind from two large Honeydew or Cantaloupe melons, and cut the flesh into small dice.

Dissolve 3½ cups of sugar in 1 cup of water in a pan over medium heat, then add the fruit and continue cooking slowly until the melon starts to become transparent. Put aside to cool.

Mix 1 tablespoon of mustard powder, 2 tablespoons of ground ginger, ½ a teaspoon of salt and 2 tablespoons of cornflour (cornstarch) with 1½ cups of apple cider or wine vinegar. Bring to the boil, stirring constantly, until the liquid thickens, then stir in the syrup and melon. Pour into warm sterilised jars.
Vegan, gluten free

Mango chutney
This is easy to prepare and makes a beautiful accompaniment to any curry or to cheese and biscuits.

Put 2 tablespoons of vegetable oil in a pan over medium heat and sauté half a finely chopped onion – preferably red – and 1 crushed clove of garlic, stirring all the time, until the onion is soft.

Add the flesh of 3 peeled and chopped mangoes, a teaspoon of cardamom seeds (or powdered cardamom), a good pinch of red chilli flakes, a good pinch of powdered ginger, ½ a cup of sugar, ½ a cup of vinegar, ¼ teaspoon of salt and a cup of water.

Simmer over a very low heat for 20-30 minutes until the chutney begins to thicken, adding more water if necessary. Pour into warm sterilised jars.
Vegan, gluten free

Mint jelly
It's not easy to find in France. Mint sauce is no problem, but jelly is limited to specialist British shops. I tried many recipes to make my own, as mint grows all over our garden, but all the results using natural pectin from apples were far too sweet, because they need too much sugar. This recipe comes from www.seaweedrecipes.co.nz and gives an excellent flavour and texture without being overly sweet.

Bring 2 cups of organic apple juice to the boil, and add 2 cups of mint leaves. Leave to simmer very slowly for 30 minutes, then strain the liquid into a clean pan and discard the leaves. Make up the liquid to 2 cups, adding a little water if necessary, and divide equally between two bowls. Leave to cool to room temperature, then sprinkle 3 teaspoons of agar agar into one of the bowls of liquid.

Bring the second bowl of juice, together with 1¼ cups of apple cider vinegar and 1 cup of sugar to the boil, stirring until the sugar has dissolved and then simmer for 20 minutes. Lower the heat, add the remaining juice with the agar agar, and bring back to the boil for two minutes.

Allow to cool until the jelly starts to thicken, then stir in 1 cup of finely chopped fresh mint and pour into warm sterilised jars.

Note: This will have more of an amber colour than commercial mint jelly, so if you want it bright green, you will need to add some green food colouring.
Vegan, gluten free

13

A Few Words About Equipment

My inner collectomaniac means that I'm a sucker for any kind of kitchen gadget, and have cupboards full of items I don't use but thought I couldn't live without.

I don't own a microwave, but I find a table-top halogen oven really useful and far quicker and more economical than using the oven for roasting, grilling, baking small amounts and heating plates.

Essentials
Cast iron frying pans and casseroles – practical, healthy and will last a lifetime
Food processor
Electric whisk
Hand blender
Salad spinner
Electric spice grinder – when I use mortar and pestle everything leaps out and runs away
Sandwich toaster – essential for making 'false samosas'
Yoghurt maker – we eat a lot of yoghurt, and I like making our own with full cream milk and milk powder to produce a nice thick Greek-style yoghurt. I know you can make it easily enough in a wide-mouthed thermos, but I like the little individual glass pots with their neat plastic lids.

A recent purchase is a fairly large electric tabletop grill that opens out so you can either grill on one side at a time, or both sides at once. We're not very adept at barbecues; in fact Terry set himself on fire and was badly burned, so the grill comes in very useful for vegetables, fish and toasted sandwiches. (Oh, just realised I can dispense with the sandwich toaster now!)

Seldom used, but I like knowing they are there.
Slow cooker – too slow – I can't think that far ahead.
Rice cooker – takes up too much room. A saucepan works just as well.
Pressure cooker – comes in handy sometimes.
Pasta maker – takes too long, makes too much mess, results not always the way I hope, and the dogs try to lick the pasta hanging up to dry.
Bread maker – I go through phases of using it.
Electric toaster – useful when we have guests and need a heap of toast, but I prefer the cast-iron frying pan.

Never!
Deep fat fryer – ugh. Couldn't bear all the sticky burned-on grease. I prefer to use a simple, cheap wok (not non-stick).
Waffle iron — it broke, haven't replaced it because we don't really eat waffles.
Ice cream maker – couldn't make it work very often, and it took more effort and time than my simple method.
Chocolate fountain – Eew!
Steamer – a colander over a pan of water does the trick.

I hope you may have found at least one or two new recipes to enjoy, and that I have correctly calculated all the conversions into cups and spoons. If I've made any slips, I apologise – please let me know and I'll correct them.

Bon Appetit!

SUSIE KELLY

Born a Londoner, Susie Kelly spent most of the first 25 years of her life in Kenya, and now lives in south-west France with her husband and assorted animals. She's slightly scatterbrained and believes that compassion, courage and a sense of humour are the three essentials for surviving life in the 21st century. She gets on best with animals, eccentrics, and elderly people.

CONNECT WITH SUSIE

Blog:
http://nodamnblog.wordpress.com

Facebook:
https://www.facebook.com/people/Susie-Kelly/Author

Twitter:
@SusieEnFrance

Sign up to the Susie Kelly Mailing List
http://eepurl.com/zyBFP
(Securely managed by Mailchimp, details are never, ever shared)

PICTURE CREDITS

MORE BOOKS BY SUSIE KELLY

Travels With Tinkerbelle: 6,000 Miles Around France In A Mechanical Wreck (Blackbird 2012) Join Susie, husband Terry and their two dogs on a camping trip around the circumference of France.

The Valley of Heaven and Hell: Cycling in the Shadow of Marie-Antoinette (Blackbird 2011) Novice cyclist Susie bikes 500 miles through Paris and Versailles, the battlefields of World War 1, the Champagne region and more. Ebook & paperback.

Two Steps Backward (Bantam 2004) The trials and tribulations of moving a family and many animals from the UK to a run-down smallholding in SW France. Paperback.

I Wish I Could Say I Was Sorry (Blackbird 2013)
With her usual humour and honesty, Susie recalls a 1950s childhood in post-war London's every shade of grey which contrasts vividly with the splendours of Africa. A moving and often shocking insight in to the earlier life of the bestselling travel writer.

Swallows & Robins:The Laughs & Tears Of A Holiday Home Owner (Blackbird 2012) 'Laugh out loud funny and a must read for anyone dreaming of the good life running gites in France.' The Good Life France

Best Foot Forward: A 500-Mile Walk Through Hidden France (Transworld 2000/Blackbird 2011) A touching and inspiring tale of the Texan pioneering spirit, English eccentricity, and two women old enough to know better.

The Lazy Cook (Book Two): Quick And Easy Sweet Treats (August 2015, Blackbird) The second of Susie's delightful round-ups of her favourite quick, simple, easy supper and pudding recipes, sprinkled with anecdote and humour.

Also available:

Best Foot Forward: A 500-Mile Walk Through Hidden France Audiobook (Audible, Amazon & iTunes)

The Susie Kelly Boxed Set Ebook of her 4 Blackbird-published French travel books (Amazon Kindle, iTunes, Barnes & Noble nook, Kobo, Scribd)

If you loved this book and would like to know more about becoming a **Reader Ambassador** for this title, please email us at blackbird.digibooks@gmail.com and we'll let you know how you can become a valuable, visible, part of this book's journey to a wider audience.

MORE BLACKBIRD DIGITAL BOOKS

Blackbird Digital Books

A publishing company for the digital age

We publish rights-reverted and new titles by established
quality writers alongside exciting new talent.

Email: blackbird.digibooks@gmail.com
http://blackbird-books.com
@blackbirdebooks

blackbird

121

READER AMBASSADORS

1. Frank Hubeny

2. Jacqui Brown, French Village Diaries

3. Hazel Hatswell

4. Susan Keefe